Pierre Trudeau Speaks Out on Meech Lake

DONALD JOHNSTON, EDITOR

Published in 1990 (revised) by General Paperbacks

First published in 1988 by Stoddart Publishing Co. Limited *under the title*
With a Bang, Not a Whimper: Pierre Trudeau Speaks Out

ISBN 0-7736-7244-3

Cover Design: Brant Cowie / ArtPlus Limited
Cover Photograph: Canadian Press

Printed in Canada

Contents

Preface

The saga of Meech Lake provides lessons on how *not* to amend a constitution. It may be too late for Canadians to heed the lessons because so much damage has already been done. Polarization has taken place; the battle is now of symbols, not substance; the weapons are blackmail and political terrorism. The results were predictable. Instead of unifying the country, Meech Lake has divided us; instead of strengthening the federation, Meech Lake is weakening it.

Canadians look on in dismay and mounting frustration. This country of extraordinary riches and potential should be moving towards the next century with a vision of what Canada could be. Instead, we continue to witness a sterile, bitter debate fuelled by Quebec nationalists and separatists who seek more autonomy and authority, not for Quebecers, but for Quebec politicians. With notable exceptions, politicians in other provinces are supportive, seeing advantages for themselves as provincial politicians in the proposed constitutional amendment. The future of Canada has taken a back seat to these narrow self-interests.

There is no federal political leadership speaking for Canada. Defending the national interest has been left to a few courageous provincial politicians, notably Clyde Wells, the Premier of Newfoundland.

I have waged my own war against Meech Lake since it was unveiled in May 1987. We were few at the beginning, but as a greater understanding of Meech Lake emerged, our numbers quickly grew. Today a majority of Canadians who understand Meech Lake are against it. But most still remain ignorant of its content, hapless bystanders to a power struggle between politicians seeking to exploit widespread ignorance of constitutional matters.

The escalation of political demagoguery in Quebec, repeated and amplified in English Canada by well-meaning but naive academics and journalists, has created the impression that relations between English-speaking and French-speaking Quebecers are poor and getting worse. The opposite is true. I have never seen relations as strong nor as positive between French and English Quebec. Hugh MacLennan's "Two Solitudes" are melting, like icebergs, into one common pool, with important but non-threatening residues still apparent.

Lord Durham described Canada as two nations warring in the bosom of a single state. If that were true in 1840, then it most certainly is not today. Politicians and their small supporting casts may be at war, but the people by and large are at peace. A way out of this Meech Lake nightmare is to convince its authors and supporters that Canadians will not join their parade once they see where it is going: the sundering of Canada into a cacophony of squabbling regions is not what Canadians want!

Politicians are sensitive to public opinion. Government by polls, not principles, is a political reality. Speaking across Canada to Canadian Clubs, service clubs, political organizations, business and professional groups, and in the give-and-take of radio hot lines, it was clear to me that an overwhelming majority of Canadians would reject Meech Lake were they to understand its implications. Yet even with the passage of two and a half years, millions of Canadians remain oblivious to its consequences.

So as the Meech Lake juggernaut moved forward, my mind turned to the prospect of writing a book. The nagging questions was, who would read *my* book on Meech Lake? Then as I listened to former prime minister Pierre Elliott Trudeau speaking to the Canadian Senate, I found the answer. Who better to tell the sad story of Meech Lake than Trudeau? So I decided to limit my role to editing and writing introductory and concluding remarks to provide a context for Trudeau's initial article, first published in *The Toronto Star*, his exposés before the Special Joint Committee of the House of Commons and the Senate, and subsequently before the Senate itself.

These Parliamentary presentations were delivered without written text. For the purpose of this book, Trudeau consented to review all this material, and suggested editorial changes to eliminate ambiguity and unnecessary repetition. To that limited extent only, the text differs from the public record. All titles and footnotes to Trudeau's text were added by me.

The first edition of this book had a different title, *With a Bang, Not a Whimper: Pierre Trudeau Speaks Out*. The present edition differs from the original in a number of ways. I have made modifications to the Introduction and Conclusion, but the principal changes arise from the deletion of an earlier appendix and the addition of an important postscript. It consists of a 1989 polemic in *La Presse* between Pierre Elliott Trudeau, journalist Marcel Adam, and former Parti-Québécois minister Claude Morin. This postscript contains several short essays by Trudeau never before published in English. In this exchange, Trudeau addresses and debunks myths and revisionist history surrounding the referendum debates of 1980 and the patriation of the Canadian Constitution in 1982.

Apart from these three men, a number of people have contributed to this book. I wish to thank Pierre Tremblay who volunteered time and effort to the project, as did Jennifer Sloan. Ian Stewart also reviewed my manuscript, offering helpful suggestions. Deborah Coyne and I.H. Asper made important contributions, as did Stoddart Publishing, especially Bill Hanna, Donald G. Bastian, and Frances Hanna.

In the first edition, I paid tribute to those Canadians from every part of this great and wonderful country and from all walks of life who called and wrote to express their concerns about Meech Lake and Canada's future. I wish to add thanks to those Canadians who continue to speak out and whose letters of protest appear regularly in the pages of newspapers across Canada.

DONALD JOHNSTON

MONTREAL
January 1990

Chapter One

Introduction

By Donald Johnston

When this book first appeared in the autumn of 1988, Canada was in the midst of a national election campaign dominated by the issue of a free trade agreement with the United States. Meech Lake was scarcely mentioned during that debate because both opposition leaders, John Turner and Ed Broadbent, accepted and supported this initiative of Prime Minister Brian Mulroney and Premier Robert Bourassa. Cynics would say their acceptance was founded more on political expediency than in any concern for the national interest. Both have repeatedly argued that since Quebec said "yes" to Canada in the 1980 Quebec referendum that it is now Canada's turn to say "yes" to Quebec. They and others who serve up this cliché conveniently ignore the fact that the Quebec government said "no" to Canada in 1980 while the people of Quebec said "yes." Now another Quebec government is threatening to say "no" to Canada if Meech Lake is not adopted. But what do the people of Quebec say? The most recent poll at the date of this writing suggests that 67 percent of Quebecers either do not know what Meech Lake is all about or are opposed to it.

Circumstances have changed dramatically since I wrote introductory remarks to the 1988 edition of this book. I noted then that "the constitutional proposal is quietly working its way through the amendment process, a proposal that will change the face of Canada forever." Gratefully, it is no longer working its way quietly through the process thanks to a handful of courageous provincial politicians: Manitoba's Gary Filmon and Sharon Carstairs, New Brunswick's Frank McKenna and, most recently and notably, Newfoundland's Clyde Wells. Federal politicians and leadership aspirants have abdicated their responsibility. Canada's salvation now rests with these few provincial leaders.

Meech Lake is a "pig in a poke" being sold enthusiastically by most political leaders to a largely uninformed public. At first, only a handful of Canadians in a position to influence public opinion attempted to pull this ugly pig from its poke for all to see. They enjoyed little success. The fact that ten premiers and the Prime Minister had reached agreement on a constitutional amendment seemed so remarkable that critics were seen as nit-pickers who had lost sight of the big picture of Canada painted in the dead of night in the secrecy of a Meech Lake retreat.

Then, on the morning of May 27, 1987, former prime minister Pierre Elliott Trudeau, a man who had devoted much of his private and nearly all of his public life to the concept of One Canada, spoke out.

Since his withdrawal from public life in 1984 he had kept his own counsel. He had watched from a distance, probably bemused, even pleased by much of what had transpired.

Editor's note: The 1987 Constitutional Accord consists of a preamble, a motion for a resolution to authorize an amendment to the Constitution of Canada and the 1987 Constitution Amendment itself, which is attached as a schedule to the motion. The preamble and motion for a resolution sets out, among other things, certain political agreements, such as some of the details of the proposed immigration deal between Ottawa and Quebec. The Constitution Amendment consists of seventeen sections, which set out the substantive constitutional changes that will be made to the Constitution Acts of 1867 and 1982. Wherever possible, when reference is made to a particular provision of the Accord, the relevant section of the Constitution Acts of 1867 and 1982 will be used. This, however, is not possible in the case of section 16 of the Constitution Amendment because it involves no specific amendment to the Constitution Acts of 1867 and 1982.

The virtual disappearance of the Quebec separatist move-
ment and the concomitant birth and growth of a new
self-confident Quebec with ambitions reaching far beyond
the province or the country must have given him great
satisfaction. Yes, Quebec was unfolding as it should within
the universe he had often described and which he had done
much to help create. Because Meech Lake was a categorical
denial of this new Quebec, a step backward to a unilingual
ghetto, it seemed inconceivable that no political leader
would attack it. He watched, he waited and when it was
obvious there was no leadership able or willing to defend a
vision of One Canada, he struck.

His initial attack — a hard-hitting, front-page article in
The Toronto Star — sent shock waves across the nation. For
the first time Canadians were aware that all was not well in
the "peaceable kingdom." His broadaxe cut deep into the
conscience of those who knew instinctively that Canada
would be mortally wounded by Meech Lake but who had
remained silent. One arch conservative with an abiding
dislike of Trudeau is reported to have said, "This time that
son of a bitch is right!" A majority of informed Canadians
agreed.

Unfortunately there is evidence that millions of Canadians remain totally unaware of the content of Meech Lake.
The Accord's greatest ally is ignorance, ambiguity, and
distortion; its greatest enemy knowledge, clarity, and truth.

Most political leaders preach that the adoption of the
Accord, without any change whatsoever, is necessary to
reintegrate Quebec into the Canadian constitutional family.
And Premier Bourassa adds that all other concerns about
Meech Lake must be addressed in a second round after it
is carved in stone. Could anyone familiar with Canadian
politics believe that Bourassa would make concessions in a
second round where he will hold a veto over changes that
are not acceptable to him today? This ruse on his part is
reminiscent of the fox in La Fontaine's fable, "The Fox and

the Billygoat." The fable finds a fox and a goat together at the bottom of a well. The fox convinces the goat to help him get out of the well against the fox's promise to help the goat out after him. The fox is freed. The second round never happened for the goat, nor would it happen for Canada!

This book is intended to provide knowledge of the Accord by bringing together some of Trudeau's comments on Meech Lake, based on his *Star* article and his testimonies before the Senate and combined House and Senate committees. In the case of his Parliamentary submissions, he spoke without text.

Canadians who read Trudeau's analysis in the following pages will see that with Meech Lake:

- Canada is to be partitioned into two distinct societies (deux nations) based on language and territory; Quebec will be French, the rest of Canada, English.
- Quebec will have a special status, authority to promote its distinct identity at home and abroad, and additional powers not available to other provinces. What authority remains to the federal government to deal with the social and economic challenges of Canada is also being removed.
- Canada is to become an association of provincial fiefdoms with semi-annual meetings between First Ministers to determine national objectives and policies and to strip Ottawa of whatever other authority the provinces might cherish. Meech Lake itself is a convincing beginning of that process.
- At Ottawa's expense, the provinces acquire powers in immigration, social and economic areas, appointments to the Senate and Supreme Court, and a veto for each over all major constitutional changes including the creation of new provinces. To make those gains secure, there is an amending formula that propels Canada's evolution down a one-way street to more and more decentraliza-

tion and ultimately to the destruction of the Canadian federation itself.

How could our First Ministers place our future as one nation in such jeopardy? Why did it happen?

The historical context is important. It is dealt with in some detail in Trudeau's comments in the Senate Chamber. But the reader should know that following the Quebec referendum of May 1980 when the people of Quebec rejected the "sovereignty-association" option, the federal government under Trudeau's leadership set about to renew the Canadian Constitution by bringing it home from the United Kingdom (a process known as patriation) with its own amending formula and a Charter of Rights and Freedoms for the benefit of all Canadians. (For reasons Trudeau explains, Canada did not possess legal authority to fully amend its own Constitution.) Canadians would at last be "sovereign in their own land" with guaranteed individual rights beyond the power of governments. All of this was accomplished in the Constitution Act of 1982. To no one's surprise, the separatist government of Quebec led by René Lévesque did not officially accept these constitutional arrangements although the province was legally bound and 72 of 75 MPs from Quebec supported the federal position and Quebec's status within the Canadian federation was assured. (This point was elaborated by Trudeau in his Senate appearance — see pages 57 to 62.)

However, as Trudeau had said, patriation was such a fundamental matter that unanimity was to be desired. With a Quebec government whose *raison d'être* was to take Quebec out of Canada, unanimity was impossible. Then in 1985, a Liberal government under Premier Robert Bourassa returned to power in Quebec and early in 1986 his minister of Intergovernmental Affairs, Gil Rémillard, unveiled five conditions which, if met, would enable the Bourassa government to lend its moral support to the Constitution of Canada. They were:

- The explicit recognition of Quebec as a distinct society.
- A guarantee of increased powers in matters of immigration.
- A limitation on the federal spending power.
- Recognition of a right of veto to the province of Quebec in constitutional matters.
- Participation by the Quebec government in appointing judges to the Supreme Court of Canada.

On the morning of April 30, 1987, provincial premiers and the Prime Minister closeted themselves at Meech Lake to consider Quebec's conditions. Few outsiders were optimistic they could be met in constitutional language without conferring a special status on Quebec which would destabilize the Canadian federation. But there was guarded optimism because the federal Liberal Party in a policy resolution of November 1986 had hammered out a position acceptable to Liberals from all provinces of Canada which seemed to meet Quebec's demands. Central to it was part of the preamble to the Constitution that would recognize the "distinctive character" of Quebec as the principal but not exclusive source of French language and culture in Canada.

On the night of April 30, after much exhausting dialogue between First Ministers and their officials, reminiscent of the bargaining and trade-offs of labour negotiations, Prime Minister Mulroney emerged triumphant to state that a deal had been struck. While the naive saw this as something of a miracle, the more observant quickly identified Meech Lake at best as a Pyrrhic victory for the national interest. The Prime Minister had cajoled and bribed provincial premiers into accepting Quebec's demands by giving them new jurisdiction and authority at the expense of the federal government. No premier had the wisdom to deny Samuel Butler's sage advice to "never . . . look a gift-horse in the mouth."

On June 3, 1987, the final Accord was signed by the same participants. Although some changes were made, not available when Trudeau published his initial attack, they had no effect on the substance of the April 30 agreement except to reinforce fears that the distinct society clause would prevail over the Charter of Rights and Freedoms. The changes did nothing to dispel fears that the Accord would create two Canadas based on language and territory.[1]

The First Ministers who signed the Accord undertook to obtain its passage, without amendment, through each of their respective legislatures. The generally accepted timetable requires its adoption by all the legislatures not later than June 23, 1990.

Meech Lake is pervasive, affecting every aspect of Canada's economic and social fabric. Ultimately it will determine our political geography. Thus the debate about Meech Lake is a debate about the future of Canada, the Canada which has existed for 121 years, the Canada we love and the Canada of which we are so proud. The Canadian formula for success has not been problem-free but by comparison with the rest of the world, its story is a glorious one of compassion, tolerance, diversity, and opportunity, a story which we should not rewrite without an informed national debate.

It is against this background that our former prime minister, the Right Honourable Pierre Elliott Trudeau, once more took the challenge to the Canadian people.

Chapter Two

'Say Goodbye to the Dream of One Canada'

From Pierre Trudeau's article in The Toronto Star, *May 27, 1987.*

The *real* question to be asked is whether the French Canadians living in Quebec need a provincial government with more powers than the other provinces.

I believe it is insulting to us to claim that we do. The new generation of business executives, scientists, writers, film-makers and artists of every description has no use for the siege mentality in which the elites of bygone days used to cower. The members of this new generation know that the true opportunities of the future extend beyond the boundaries of Quebec, indeed beyond the boundaries of Canada itself. They don't suffer from any inferiority complex, and they say good riddance to the times when we didn't dare to measure ourselves against "others" without fear and trembling. In short, they need no crutches.

Quite the contrary, they know that Quebecers are capable of playing a leading role within Canada and that — if we wish it — the entire country can provide us with a powerful springboard. In this, today's leaders have finally caught up to the rest of the population, which never paid much heed to inward-looking nationalism — that escape from reality in which only the privileged could afford to indulge.

Unfortunately, the politicians are the exception to the rule. And yet one would have thought that those who want to engage in politics in our province would have learned at least one lesson from the history of the last 100 years: Quebecers like strong governments, in Quebec *and in Ottawa*. And our most recent history seems to establish beyond question that if Quebecers feel well represented in Ottawa, they have only mistrust for special status, sovereignty-association and other forms of separatism. They know instinctively that they cannot hope to wield *more* power within their province, without agreeing to wield *less* in the country as a whole.

To Each, His Own Political Advantage

How, then, could 10 provincial premiers and a federal prime minister agree to designate Quebec as a "distinct society?"

It's because they all, each in his own way, saw that this accord was to their political advantage:

1: Those who have never wanted a bilingual Canada — Quebec separatists and western separatists — get their wish right in the first paragraphs of the accord, with recognition of "the existence of French-speaking Canada . . . and English-speaking Canada."

Those Canadians who fought for a single Canada, bilingual and multicultural, can say goodbye to their dream: We are henceforth to have two Canadas, each defined in terms of its language. And because the Meech Lake accord states in the same breath that "Quebec constitutes, within Canada, a distinct society" and that "the role of the legislature and government to preserve and promote (this) distinct identity . . . is affirmed," it is easy to predict what future awaits anglophones living in Quebec and what treatment will continue to be accorded to francophones living in provinces where they are fewer in number than Canadians of Ukrainian or German origin.

Indeed, the text of the accord spells it out: In the other provinces, where bilingualism still has an enormously long way to go, the only requirement is to "protect" the status quo, while in Quebec the requirement is to "promote" the distinct character of Quebec society.

In other words, the government of Quebec must take measures and its legislature must pass laws aimed at promoting the uniqueness of Quebec. And the text of the accord specifies at least one aspect of this uniqueness: "French-speaking Canada" is "centred" in that province. Thus Quebec acquires a new constitutional jurisdiction that the rest of Canada does not have: promoting the concentration of French in Quebec. It is easy to see the consequences for French and English minorities in the country, as well as for foreign policy, for education, for the economy, for social legislation, and so on.

2: Those who never wanted a Charter of Rights entrenched in the Constitution can also claim victory. Because "the Constitution of Canada shall be interpreted in a manner consistent with . . . (Quebec's) role to preserve and promote the distinct identity" of Quebec society, it follows that the courts will have to interpret the Charter in a way that does not interfere with Quebec's "distinct society" as defined by Quebec laws.

For those Canadians who dreamed of the Charter as a new beginning for Canada, where everyone would be on an equal footing and where citizenship would finally be founded on a set of commonly shared values, there is to be nothing left but tears.

3: Those who want to prevent the Canadian nation from being founded on such a community of values are not content merely to weaken the Charter: They are getting a constitutionalized — that is, irreversible — agreement "which will commit Canada to withdrawing from all services . . . regarding the reception and the integration (including linguistic and cultural integration)" of immigrants. We can guess what visions of Canada will be conveyed to immigrants in the various provinces, with Canada undertaking to foot the bill for its own balkanization, "such withdrawal to be accompanied by fair compensation."

What's more, this principle of withdrawal accompanied by "fair compensation" is to be applied to all "new shared-cost programs." That will enable the provinces to finish off the balkanization of languages and cultures with the balkanization of social services. After all, what provincial politician will not insist on distributing in his own way (what is left, really, of "national objectives?") and to the advantage of his constituents, the money he'll be getting painlessly from the federal treasury?

4: For those who — despite all the Canadian government's largesse with power and with funds — might still have been hesitant to sign the Meech Lake accord, the Prime Minister had two more surprises up his sleeve. From now on, the Canadian government won't be able to appoint anyone to the Supreme Court and the Senate except people designated by the provinces! And from now on, any province that doesn't like an important constitutional amendment will have the power to either block the passage of that amendment or to opt out of it, with "reasonable compensation" as a reward!

This second surprise gives each of the provinces a constitutional veto. And the first surprise gives them an absolute right of veto over Parliament, since the Senate will eventually be composed entirely of persons who owe their appointments to the provinces.

It also transfers the supreme judicial power to the provinces, since Canada's highest court will eventually be composed entirely of persons put forward by the provinces.

Robert Stanfield, leader of the federal Conservative Party—and Leader of the Opposition—from 1967 to 1976, endorsed the concept of "Two Nations." *(Canadian Press)*

Such Sleight of Hand!

What a magician this Mr. (Brian) Mulroney is, and what a sly fox! Having forced Mr. Bourassa (Quebec Premier Robert Bourassa) to take up his responsibilities on the world stage, having obliged him to sit alongside the Prime Minister of Canada at summit conferences where francophone heads of state and heads of government discuss *international* economics and politics, he also succeeds in obliging him to pass laws promoting the "distinct character" of Quebec.

Likewise having enjoined Mr. Peckford (Newfoundland Premier Brian Peckford) to preside over the management of Canadian seabeds (offshore resources), having compelled Mr. Getty (Alberta Premier Don Getty) to accept the dismantling of Canadian energy policy, having convinced Mr. Peterson (Ontario Premier David Peterson) to take up his responsibilities in the negotiation of an international free trade treaty, having promised jurisdiction over fisheries to the East and reform of the Senate to the West, Mr. Mulroney also succeeds in imposing on all these fine folks the heavy burden of choosing senators and Supreme Court justices! And all this without even having to take on the slightest extra task for the Canadian government, be it national regulation of securities markets, be it the power to strengthen the Canadian common market, be it even the repeal of the overriding ("notwithstanding") clause of the Charter.[2]

In a single master stroke, this clever negotiator has thus managed to approve the call for Special Status (Jean Lesage and Claude Ryan), the call for Two Nations (Robert Stanfield), the call for a Canadian Board of Directors made up of 11 first ministers (Allan Blakeney and Marcel Faribeault), and the call for a Community of Communities (Joe Clark).

He has not quite succeeded in achieving the separatist party's *sovereignty-association*, but he has put Canada on the fast track for getting there. It doesn't take a great thinker to predict that the political dynamic will draw the best people to the provincial capitals, where the real power will reside,

Marcel Faribeault, prominent Montreal notary and a staunch
Canadian nationalist. He was an outspoken proponent of a special
status for the province of Quebec, both as an advisor on
constitutional matters to Daniel Johnson, and as the architect of the
"Two Nations" theory of Canada that the federal Conservatives
adopted to fight the 1968 general election. Faribeault was also a
prestige Conservative candidate in a Montreal riding in that election
which saw him defeated and Trudeau's "One Canada" theme bring
Trudeau a landslide victory.   *(Canadian Press)*

while the federal capital will become a backwater for political and bureaucratic rejects.

The School of Blackmail

What a dark day for Canada was this April 30, 1987! In addition to surrendering to the provinces important parts of its jurisdiction (the spending power, immigration), in addition to weakening the Charter of Rights, the Canadian state made subordinate to the provinces its legislative power (Senate) and its judicial power (Supreme Court). And it did this without hope of ever reversing the process (a constitutional veto granted to each one of the provinces). It even committed itself to a constitutional "second round" at which the demands of the provinces already dominate the agenda.[3]

All this was done under the pretext of "permitting Quebec to fully participate in Canada's constitutional evolution." As if Quebec had not, right from the beginning, fully participated in Canada's constitutional evolution!

More than a half-dozen times since 1927, Quebec and the other provinces tried together with the Canadian government to "repatriate" our Constitution and to agree on an amending formula.

"Constitutional evolution" presupposed precisely that Canada would have its Constitution and would be able to amend it. Yet almost invariably, it was the Quebec provincial government that had blocked the process. Thus, in 1965, Mr. Lesage and his minister at the time, Mr. Rene Levesque, withdrew their support from the Fulton-Favreau formula (a plan to amend the British North America Act) after they had accepted and defended it.[4] And Mr. Bourassa, who in Victoria in 1971 had proposed a formula which gave Quebec a right of absolute veto over all constitutional amendments, withdrew his own endorsement 10 days after the conference.[5] In both cases, the reason for backing off was the same: Quebec would "permit" Canada to Canadianize the colonial

Joe Clark, prime minister of Canada in 1979-1980. Clark promoted the notion of a "Community of Communities" as a concept of Canada and was dubbed the "head waiter" by Pierre Trudeau for serving the interests of provincial premiers rather than the national interest of the people of Canada. *(Canadian Press)*

document that served as our Constitution, only if the rest of Canada granted Quebec a certain "special status."

The result was that 10 years later, when the Canadian government tried once again to restart the process of constitutional evolution, it faced the roadblock of 10 provinces which all wanted their own "special status"; inevitably, they had enrolled in the school of blackmail of which Quebec was the founder and top-ranking graduate.[6]

The rest of the story is well known. The Canadian government declared that it would bypass the provinces and present its constitutional resolution in London. The Supreme Court acknowledged that this would be legal but that it wouldn't be nice.[7] The Canadian government made an effort at niceness that won the support of nine provinces out of 10. Mr. Levesque, knowing that a constitutional deal would interfere with the progress of separatism, played for broke, refused to negotiate and turned again to the Supreme Court to block "the process of constitutional evolution." He lost his gamble: The court declared not only that Quebec had no right of veto[8] (Mr. Bourassa had in any event rejected it after Victoria, and Mr. Levesque had lost it somewhere in the west of the country), but also that Quebec was fully a party to "Canada's constitutional evolution."

A gamble lost, a gamble won — big deal! Quebec public opinion, with its usual maturity, applauded the players and then, yawning, turned to other matters.

But not the Quebec nationalists! Imagine: They had tried blackmail once again, but Canada had refused to pay. It was more than a lost gamble, it was "an attack in force" (political science professor Leon Dion and many others), it was "a slap in the face to Quebec" (Paul-Andre Comeau, assistant editor of *Le Devoir*). Because in addition to being perpetual losers, the nationalists are sore losers. For example, *they* didn't lose the 1980 referendum: *The people* made a mistake, or were fooled by the federal government. Likewise, after Robert Bourassa and Rene Levesque had foolishly passed up a right of veto for Quebec, it was necessary to somehow blame it on the federal government: attack in force, slap in the face!

The provincializing politicians, whether they sit in Ottawa or in Quebec, are also perpetual losers; they don't have the stature or the vision to dominate the Canadian stage, so they need a Quebec ghetto as their lair. If they didn't have the sacred rights of French Canadians to defend against the rest of the world, if we could count on the Charter and the courts for that, they would lose their reason for being. That is why they are once again making common cause with the Quebec nationalists to demand special status for Quebec.

That bunch of snivellers should simply have been sent packing and been told to stop having tantrums like spoiled adolescents. But our current political leaders lost their nerve. By rushing to the rescue of the unhappy losers, they hope to gain votes in Quebec; in reality, they are only flaunting their political stupidity and their ignorance of the demographic data regarding nationalism.

Bringing It All Back Home?

It would be difficult to imagine a more complete bungle.

Mr. Bourassa, who had been elected to improve the economic and political climate in the province, chose to flail around on the one battlefield where the Pequistes have the advantage: that of the nationalist bidding war. Instead of turning the page on Mr. Levesque's misadventures, he wanted to espouse them. Instead of explaining to people that, thanks to the ineptitude of the Pequistes we were fully bound by the Constitution of 1982, Mr. Bourassa preferred to embrace the cause of the "moderate" nationalists.

Well, good luck! The Pequistes will never stop preaching that the Meech Lake accord enshrines the betrayal of Quebec's interests. And a person as well-informed as (newspaper columnist) Lysianne Gagnon was able to twit Mr. Bourassa

Louis St. Laurent (left) is congratulated by Mackenzie King following his becoming prime minister; November 1948.   *(Chris Lund; National Film Board/Public Archives Canada)*

thus: "Quebec didn't achieve even a shadow of special status . . . the other provinces fought tooth and nail for the sacrosanct principle of equality. And they too will have everything Quebec asked for!" (*La Presse*, May 2, 1987). Does not the very nature of immaturity require that "the others" not get the same "trinkets" as we?

The possibility exists, moreover, that in the end Mr. Bourassa, true to form, will wind up repudiating the Meech Lake accord, because Quebec will still not have gotten enough.[9] And that would inevitably clear the way for the real saviours: the separatists.

As for Mr. Mulroney, he had inherited a winning hand.

During the earlier attempts to Canadianize the Constitution, prime ministers Mackenzie King, St. Laurent, Diefenbaker, Pearson and Trudeau[10] had *acted as if* it couldn't be done without the unanimous consent of the provinces. That gave the provinces a considerable advantage in the negotiations and accounted for the concessions that the Canadian prime ministers had to contemplate in each round of negotiations. It is likely, for instance, that if King had been prepared to accept unanimity (Mulroney-style) as the amending formula, the Constitution could have been repatriated as early as 1927.

But since 1982, Canada had its Constitution, including a Charter which was binding on the provinces as well as the federal government. From then on, the advantage was on the Canadian government's side; it no longer had anything very urgent to seek from the provinces; it was they who had become the supplicants. From then on, "Canada's constitutional evolution" could have taken place without preconditions and without blackmail, on the basis of give and take among equals. Even a united front of the 10 provinces could not have forced the federal government to give ground: with the assurance of a creative equilibrium between the provinces and the central government, the federation was set to last a thousand years!

Prime Minister Brian Mulroney and the premiers after they had reached constitutional agreement at Meech Lake, Quebec, April 30, 1987.   *(Canadian Press)*

The Unforeseen Eventuality

Alas, only one eventuality had not been foreseen: that one day the government of Canada might fall into the hands of a wimp. It has now happened. And the Right Honorable Brian Mulroney, PC, MP, with the complicity of 10 provincial premiers, has already entered into history as the author of a constitutional document which — if it is accepted by the people and their legislators — will render the Canadian state totally impotent. That would destine it, given the dynamics of power, to be governed eventually by eunuchs.

Chapter Three

'There Must Be a Sense of Belonging'

Pierre Trudeau's presentation to the Joint Committee of the House of Commons and Senate.

The Right Honourable Pierre Elliott Trudeau (Individual Presentation): Mr. Chairman, ladies and gentlemen, first I want to thank you for having invited me. I appreciate the occasion of presenting my ideas.

As I told you, Mr. Chairman, I am not going to submit a brief. As you say, my ideas are generally known as regards the Constitution, so I will only briefly run through the various objections I have to the Meech Lake and Langevin Block accords, and then I would be happy to submit to questions or whatever discussion ensues.

I do not have much to read, but I did want to start with a quote.

I will therefore begin by quoting two of the most brilliant parliamentarians Canada has ever known. Edward Blake, some half-dozen years after the beginning of Confederation, said:

> The future of Canada depends very largely upon the cultivation of a national spirit. We must find some common ground on which to unite, some common aspiration to be shared, and I think it can be found alone in the cultivation of that national spirit to which I have referred.

Henri Bourassa, Canadian nationalist, politician and journalist who founded *Le Devoir*. Grandson of Louis-Joseph Papineau, hero of the 1837 rebellion, Bourassa was truly a Pan-Canadian nationalist, abhorring the semi-colonial ties to Britain but equally opposed to the notion of a separate French-Canadian state, a concept embraced by French-Canadian nationalists. *(Public Archives Canada)*

And, almost half a century later, the great Henri Bourassa observed that there was, in Canada, a distinctive patriotism among people living in Ontario, another in Quebec, and yet another among Westerners. But, he said, "there is no Canadian patriotism; and as long as we have no Canadian patriotism, there will be no Canadian nation."

Essentially, Mr. Chairman, I propose to assess the various provisions of the accord in light of those two quotations — in the light of what Bourassa called Canadian patriotism and what Blake called the national spirit . . . Of course, the expression "Canadian patriotism", and even more so "provincial patriotism" may seem a little passé these days, but I do not believe I am misinterpreting them if I say that what they had in mind was that there must be, in relation to one's country and its people, a greater loyalty than the sum of the loyalties towards the provinces. In other words, there is a Canadian common good that is broader than the common good of all of the provinces. There must be some sense of belonging to one nation in order to cultivate the national spirit; there must be an attachment to the larger entity we call Canada — an attachment somewhat less sentimental, more rational and broader than mere loyalty to each of the individual provinces. In short, Blake and Bourassa, as I see it, wanted the "Canadian entity" to consist of more than simply the sum of all the provinces.

Starting from that, I would like to remind the members of the committee of the assessment made by the actual observers, including the First Ministers, the day after the accords were reached. There was talk of massive or extensive decentralization; of the accord representing the greatest victory for the provinces since Confederation. And particularly in provincial quarters, much was made of the fact that this represented a triumph for provincial patriotism. But I believe it is more than a triumph for provincial patriotism.

The Very Essence of the Canadian Federation

In my view, and I begin by looking at three of the amendments — the proposed changes strike at what is, in fact, the very essence of the Canadian federation. They undermine the three fundamental components of any modern democratic state: executive power, legislative power and judicial power. They undermine and eat away at our Canadian sovereignty, by placing the three fundamental divisions of the modern state under the remote control of the provinces. Firstly, in the case of the legislative power, our Canadian Parliament is of course made up of two legislative bodies, the Senate and the House of Commons, the House of Commons being an elected body, and the Senate one, up until now, appointed by the federal government. Henceforth, members of the Senate will have to have been nominated by the provinces.[11] In other words, the national government, acting on behalf of the Canadian state, loses its ability to choose those who will sit in one of our legislative chambers, both of which, as we well know, are absolutely essential for the passage of all legislation. A veto by the Senate, commandeered by the provinces, which are assured of the loyalty of their senators, would be enough to ensure that no federal legislation could be passed.

Secondly, the mechanism for the Supreme Court is the same;[12] only those nominated by the provinces will be appointed to that body. So, once again, provincial governments will be exercising remote control over a body which, thus far, has been entirely the responsibility of the federal government. The Accord transfers that aspect of Canadian sovereign power to the provinces.

Thirdly, in the case of the executive,[13] we note that there will henceforth be two federal-provincial conferences held annually from now until eternity, as long as Canada remains a nation; a conference on the Constitution and constitutional affairs in general; another on economic and other matters.

Edward Blake became leader of the Ontario Liberal Party in 1868 and in 1871, the second premier of that province. Entering federal politics, he became a minister in Alexander Mackenzie's government, succeeding Mackenzie as leader. After two electoral defeats he resigned in 1887. A strong Canadian nationalist, he is said to be responsible for attracting to politics such prominent Liberals and statesmen as Oliver Mowat and Wilfrid Laurier. *(William J. Topley; National Archives of Canada)*

These federal-provincial conferences are, per se, a good thing in a federation. But to have two per year forced on us by the Constitution itself, particularly in the light of what happened at Meech Lake and in the Langevin building, and what has been announced as an agenda for the federal-provincial conference to be held next year, leads us to believe that Canada's destiny henceforth will be ordained by a permanent conference composed of one Prime Minister speaking on Canada's behalf, and ten premiers speaking on behalf of their individual provinces. So, either it will be 10 against 1, in which case, the odds are that the weight of the majority will be enough to bring the federal Prime Minister onside; or else we will have a *directoire* lording it over our federal and provincial Parliament and legislatures.

But let us not forget that in contrast to the federal state, the legislatures and the provincial executives, will continue to be completely autonomous in governing their own affairs. There is in addition an interprovincial conference[14] held every year where provincial premiers meet. The federal government is never invited to such meetings, because the provinces do not want the federal government to come and stick its nose in provincial affairs. However, the reverse will not be true because of this new amendment.

So, I repeat, these three amendments weaken — I can find no other appropriate term — federal sovereign power. And certainly, it is glaringly obvious that in no way do they point in the direction that Henri Bourassa referred to, when he spoke of Canadian patriotism; they are certainly not likely to cultivate the national spirit without which, Edward Blake felt, there could be no Canadian nation.

Provincialism: A Community of Communities

Apart from the arguments suggesting that Canada is moving towards a kind of community of communities, a sort of confederation or directory of 11 First Ministers getting together to try and determine what direction the entire country — not just the provinces, but the entire country — should take, there are four amendments whose specific aim is to work very strongly in favour of provincialism.

Let us begin with the amendment on immigration.[15] Canadians who have come from other countries arrive here, I believe — at least the majority — wanting to become part of a great country called Canada. Yet henceforth, because of the constitutional accords, they can be received by any of the provinces, and certainly will be received by one particular province interested in integrating these immigrants into the Quebec state and having them establish themselves there.

Let us just take the example of the Province of Quebec. It is this province that lobbied most to have this amendment accepted. The Province of Quebec, by its own statutes, recognizes one official language, the French language. Our Canadian laws recognize two official languages in section 16 of the Charter, English and French; those are the official languages of Canada.

I do not think one has to stretch one's imagination much to see that provincial officials will be inclined to tell immigrants that they are living in a province where there is only one official language, rather than in a country where there are in fact two; and that the Province of Quebec, which constitutes a distinct society — and I will go into that further later on — is different. I am not saying they will be taught nonsense, or that this is a sin; I am simply saying that it seems quite clear the notion of provincial patriotism will become stronger. The same will apply to Newfoundland and British Columbia, minus that linguistic difference.

In effect, the reception and integration of immigrants will be in the hands of provincial officials who will no longer be subject to the federal government's overview . . . that is another thing that must be stressed with respect to these amendments. They are taking us in a direction from which there will be no turning back. These are not simply administrative arrangements of which there have been so many since the beginning of our Confederation. Nor are they statutory agreements, of which there have also been many and because of which, throughout a certain period of our history, the pendulum swung towards a greater centralization, as was the case during the war and post-war periods; at other times, the pendulum swung towards greater decentralization. And this has certainly been the case in Canada since at least 1955 or 1960, I would say; for administrative and sometimes statutory reasons, we have been moving towards increased power for the provinces since that time. We have only to compare federal and provincial budget estimates to realize that.

And there will be no turning back;[16] once these amendments have been ratified, the provinces, with their provincialist views, will be in charge . . . and there will be a price to pay. Once again, this is not necessarily a criticism of the provincial premiers; it is their job to try and get more powers, more money, more jurisdiction and what have you for their provinces. All politicians — and you are politicians — think they can govern better than anyone else; provincial politicians are no exception. So, the more they can grab for themselves, the more we will see provincialism developing at the expense of what Henri Bourassa called national patriotism, without which, he said, there could be no Canadian nation.

What About the National Patriotism?

So much for the amendment on immigration; one could almost say the same about the amendment to federal spending powers. We all know the spending power[17] is a powerful means of developing a sense of national belonging. Whether we are talking about health insurance or the various social assistance schemes funded jointly by the federal government and the provinces, all these plans or schemes are brought into being by the federal government under the Consititution, and they are good for Canadian patriotism because they give Canadians a sense of belonging to one nation. So, whether we are Quebeckers or Albertans, we have the guarantee that wherever we go, we will be protected by a similar health insurance plan.

But once — under the present constitutional proposals — every province is in a position to receive compensation rather than be part of the national scheme, it will be perfectly natural for a politician to say: well, thank you very much; I will take the money you get from federal taxes and spend it as I see fit. And once again, it means an even greater tendency, a greater weight on the side of provincialism, at the expense of a federal institution or legislation which, up until now, has given Canadians a feeling of belonging to one Canada. In the same way the Canadian Charter of Rights and Freedoms was important to Canadian unity, as were the patriation of the Constitution and the new Canadian flag. All of those things are important in the sense that they help Canadians to realize that they share with *all* other Canadians, *throughout* the country, the same set of fundamental values.

And once we start attacking those fundamental values, well, people will start saying: "We can do it just as well our own way", say in Alberta or Ontario, when it comes to administering the health insurance plan. And that may be true, particularly in wealthy provinces. But we are again destroying a chance to create the national will, or the national patriotism I have referred to.

The next example I wish to mention, and I still have two amendments to deal with, is the formula for amending the Constitution.[18] Well, the least we can say about the new formula being proposed is that whatever consensus there may be in Canada, however broad be the general will of Canadians to strike out in new directions, however broad that consensus, we will never be able to take Canada in that direction if one province is opposed to it. Were 25 million Canadians to express a national will on an important issue, it would only take 100,000 Canadians saying "No, you will not take that direction'' to prevent us from doing it. Again, I am not saying that Prince Edward Island, since it is to that province that I refer, or even Newfoundland, or Quebec, or Manitoba would necessarily be wrong, I am simply suggesting that Meech Lake will allow people to say: "Yes, we have our own provincial patriotism back home." It is a case of the interest of one province coming before the common good of all Canada. And that was certainly not the wish of Henri Bourassa when he said: We will have to create a Canadian nation by developing Canadian patriotism.

Finally, I come to what is perhaps the most important point of all: the one dealing with Quebec as a distinct society.[19] I hasten to say right from the outset that this is indeed a sociological reality, and that I see no harm in our thinking it to be true, or even expressing the thought verbally or in writing, if we so choose. But let us also recognize right from the start that when we talk about a distinct society, and particularly when we enshrine that into the Constitution as an operative clause, we are, by definition, by the actual meaning of the terms, working towards or promoting a provincialist view of Canada. Not national patriotism, not the national spirit that Blake was talking about!

Is that regrettable or not? Time will tell. But certainly, if that amendment is added to all the others, you have a massive shift towards provincial patriotisms, towards the idea that Canada is a nice "country," but it is made up of a collection of provinces, no more no less, and that our provincial loyalties will be enough to hold us together as one nation.

Well, many people do not think so, and I am one of them. I think that if we want to have a federal and not a confederal country, we have to have a national government, a national parliament that can speak for all Canadians, since the House of Commons is indeed the only legislature in the country whose members are elected by all Canadians rather than by separate regions called provinces.

Just a word to conclude, Mr. Chairman. I do not want to go into the legal technicalities — that awful word — but perhaps I shall do so if I am asked to during the discussion; I just want to ask a fairly obvious question. Does putting this definition of Quebec as a distinct society into the interpretative formula, section 2 of the British North America Act, have a constitutional effect? It is a sociological fact, all right, agreed, but is there a constitutional effect? Is it meant to be an interpretative principle which will lead the courts to read the rest of the Constitution in terms of this distinct society?

I shall take you back to Philosophy I and put a logical alternative to you. Either the phrase "distinct society" means nothing, or it means something. If it is meaningless, I find it rather insulting and I think that is the opinion, if I read the documents correctly, that Senator Murray presented to this committee. If this phrase is meaningless, has no constitutional impact, well, it is rather insulting for Quebec to be told, "Okay, you are a distinct society, but you shall have no more powers than the others, basically you are no more distinct than the others." Because Newfoundland also claims to be a distinct province, and certainly British Columbia and many others. So you Quebeckers will be told that you constitute a distinct society, but do not count on the Constitution to give you powers to preserve or develop or protect this distinct society.

When you are told in subsection 3 of section 2:

> The role of the legislature and government of Quebec to preserve and promote the distinct identity of Quebec . . . is affirmed.

all you are being told is that it is your duty, your role, to govern the province well. The other provinces do not have to be told that, because they are sensible enough to govern themselves properly without being told.

But you Quebeckers are a distinct society, and it is the Government of Quebec's role to govern that province well. No special powers, nothing extra goes with that; it is just a statement of sociological reality which would apply to any other province.

Well, all I can tell you, ladies and gentlemen, is that if you take that view of the interpretative clause, you are in for some nasty surprises later on. Because you just have to read what the representatives of the Quebec government have said to their constituents publicly, in the National Assembly and in the newspapers. They see things differently; they feel that if the lawmakers, and all the more so the Constitution writers, say something, they want their words to have meaning. And personally, I cannot blame Quebeckers for thinking so. It is an old legal principle that legislators do not engage in empty rhetoric. That can happen, but not when writing laws.

Thus, we have to examine the hypothesis that "distinct society" means something. And what does it mean? Obviously there is much disagreement about that. You have only to read the testimony of some people, of the Premier of Quebec, of his Minister of Intergovernmental Affairs, Mr. Rémillard, and you will see that they give it a pretty broad meaning.

Apply the distinct society clause to the Canadian Charter of Rights, for example. The crucial importance of the Charter meant that we all share a set of common values and that all Canadians are thence on an equal footing; whether they be Quebeckers, Albertans, French, English, Jewish, Hindu, they all have the same rights. No one is special. All Canadians are equal, and that equality flows from the Charter.

As soon as you say, "Well, Quebec is unique under the Constitution, we can administer ourselves, we do not need this Charter". . . and I think that is the effect of the distinct society clause . . . what do you do? You eat away and undermine further the Canadian spirit that is so essential to unity, as Blake told us.

Peace . . . But at What Price?

There. In conclusion, Mr. Chairman, I can just say that the future may not be as peaceful as the present. It was said after the Accord that finally peace had been restored to federal-provincial relations. Yes, peace! But at what price? Did the federal government somewhere, with a few commas or ellipsis points, obtain one iota of additional power? The answer is no. Did the provinces receive powers? Well, everything I just named gives more power to the provinces.

So, we have made peace, but how? First, by giving the provinces everything they wanted. I assure you that I could have had peace, that Mackenzie King could have had peace with the provinces, that John A. Macdonald could have had peace with the provinces, if they had given them everything they asked for. So that peace has been dearly bought. And I predict that it will be a temporary peace, because the next federal-provincial conference already has on its agenda further transfers of powers to the provinces, Newfoundland in particular. All the provinces will say, "Me too, gimme!" And that will be the story in the future: Provincialism triumphant.

Second, we have made peace with Quebec by letting it believe that "distinct society" means Two Nations. If the courts hold that it does have that meaning, Canada is doomed. If they hold otherwise, Quebec will have been tricked, and the howls of protest will strengthen separatism. One way or another, Meech Lake may mean the peace of the grave for the Canada we know and love.

Chapter Four

'We, the People of Canada'

Pierre Trudeau's testimony to the Senate Submissions Group on the Meech Lake Constitutional Accord.

Right Hon. Pierre Elliott Trudeau, P.C.: Thank you, Mr. Chairman.

I would like to say, first of all, that today I intend to speak mostly in English, since before the Special Joint Committee of the Senate in the House of Commons I spoke mainly in French. Of course during question period, if there is one, I should be happy to use either official language.

I would like to say that I am extremely happy to appear before the Senate for a variety of reasons. I have been given by you, Mr. Chairman, a generous amount of time. Constitution discussion can be sometimes tedious, but can also be interesting. For my part, I thought that rather than get into legal technicalities, which I did, to a certain extent, when I appeared before the joint committee, I would try to put the discussion in historical perspective, show the dynamic forces which are at work in building a country, and try to draw conclusions as to where this particular 1987 Constitutional Accord might lead us.

The Place for Sober Second Thought

I am also happy to be in the Senate, because it is the place for sober second thought, and it is my impression that neither the First Ministers nor the members of the House of Commons, for reasons of their own, were able to go into that sober second thinking. The First Ministers because there was a certain amount of euphoria at having "brought Quebec into the Constitution," as the expression goes. Therefore, they had a reluctance to look back and say, "Well, we might have made some mistakes and we should correct them" — something, mind you, that was done after the agreement of November 5, 1981. Senators will recall that in those 1981 negotiations we had dropped a clause on the protection of equality of the sexes and a clause on the aboriginals. After the agreement was signed, it was still possible to put those clauses in without destroying the agreement.

As to the House of Commons today, well, it is well known that the three political parties, lest they be accused of offending Quebec, did not want to re-open the accord. Therefore, the second thought, though it might have existed, was not translated into action in the House of Commons.

Incidentally, I think that in itself is a reason to argue that special status or distinct society, or whatever you want to call it, is not really necessary for Quebec. Politically, the importance of Quebec in making or breaking governments is so great that the three political parties did not dare vote the slightest amendment to the accord lest the Government of Quebec, and, perhaps, the people, would not like it. In that sense, then, Quebec *has* a special status in the Constitution by its electoral force. The reluctance of the House of Commons was, I think, also slightly futile, since I have no evidence that in the polls, at any rate, there was a surge of support for those who had initiated the Meech Lake Accord.

But the danger of not having second thoughts is that that can bring Parliament into disrepute. That is why I am glad that the Senate will compensate for any second thought that hasn't been in evidence in the House of Commons.

Legislators by profession, if I can say that, are supposed to look at the bills or resolutions, the projects that are put before them, with a view to improvement, if they see faults. It is not expected that they should vote them as they are. If legislators see contradictions or inconsistencies, it is their role to move and vote on amendments. It is a laughable proposition to think that a legislator could be told, "Well, pass the bill, imperfect as it is — you will get some other chance in some other bill to correct it." Yet, in a constitutional matter, where the second chance is very unlikely ever to arise because of the rigidity of the amending procedure, this is what the House of Commons has decided to do — pass a resolution with its known imperfections, its known contradictions or known vaguenesses which will have to be interpreted, and make no effort to correct them. In that regard, I must say that in reading the joint committee report[20] I was surprised to see at page 51 that that committee calmly envisaged that minority rights under the Charter might be diminished, yet made no recommendations for clarifying or changing that. The report says:

> In law, the distinct society clause is *unlikely* to erode in any *significant* way the existing constitutional rights of the English-speaking minority within Quebec.

Well, as far as reassurances go, that is not the strongest one I have ever heard — "unlikely in any significant way to erode." It would seem to me that this is a clear case where, at least, every party would have been able to agree or, perhaps, not to agree, but then we would know that the accord was built on a misunderstanding.

The third reason I am happy to be here is that it is the role of the Senate to maintain a balance within the federation. That is usually understood as protecting the provinces. That is the role of the second or upper chambers in most federations. In that regard, many of you will recall that that was what was done in this chamber in 1978, when Bill C-60 purported to make some changes to the Senate. The Senate really threatened obstruction until we had a clarification of whether such changes could legally be made by the federal government alone. The government complied, and we sent Bill C-60 to the Supreme Court on a reference. We were told that, in fact, the Senate had been justified in casting doubts on that proposal.

I suggest that in the case of the 1987 accord we are also in a situation where the Senate should be ensuring balance in the federation. This is an accord which transfers large amounts of power from the central government to the provinces. I think I will have time to go into that later on, but since no signing premier is prepared to speak for Canada, nor is any federal political party, and even the Queen herself is forced to say that the accord is a good thing, it seems to me that if balance is to be brought, it should be brought by this house. This Senate can become a focal point for the most important constitutional debate or certainly one of the most important, in this period of our history.

Finally, the reason I am happy to be here is that the father of the accord, the Minister for Federal-Provincial Relations[21] in this government, sits in this place. I am not sure if he is here or not, but I feel that the debate can be joined in this house between those who support and those who do not support the accord. So far we have had something like a dialogue of the deaf. Some experts have appeared before the joint committee and before this house, arguing that this was good or bad, that this was clear or not clear, and that this had effect or did not have effect. But here is a place where I think we can discuss the thing together, where we can ask each other questions — I hope there will be time for that.

Sir John A. Macdonald, the first prime minister of Canada and first in a long line of federal leaders concerned about the proper balance of powers between federal and provincial governments. *(National Archives of Canada)*

If Senator Murray is not here today, he might be here tomorrow, and, in a sense, it will be another dialogue of the deaf, but I feel he and I have already begun our dialogue. I did publish a letter in *La Presse* and in the English press on May 27, 1987. Senator Murray, on May 30, just three days later, replied to my letter, in the *Globe and Mail*. I had expressed some mild reservations about the accord, and the senator answered in kind with, I must say, a very good letter. I say this without any sarcasm. I have, really, no disagreement on facts that he used in his letter and very few, though perhaps major disagreements, on opinions. So it was a good letter, and I think I will use it as a theme for the rest of the discussion.

In a sense, Senator Murray alleged that the November 5, 1981, agreement was flawed because it had a dark side — ''un côté ténébreux'' is what he said in French, arising from three points. First, obviously, Quebec had not signed that agreement. Second, there was an opting out provision[22] in the amending formula, which I, myself, had denounced as bad, yet, here it was. Third, there was a notwithstanding clause,[23] which I also believed was bad and which remained in the Charter.

I want to show in the rest of this presentation how those flaws came about. That means going into the history of the negotiations to a certain extent. I then want to show how those clauses, far from being corrected in the 1987 accord, were made infinitely worse. Finally, towards the conclusion, I would like to suggest what can be done by the Senate, by the provinces and by the people to prevent irreparable damage to Canada's integrity.

The Path to Full Nationhood

Dealing with the history of this whole matter, I will not say anything about the earlier years, except to remind everyone of what they know. From John A. Macdonald's day on, the history of federal-provincial relations in Canada has been one

At the Dominion-Provincial Conference in Ottawa, November 1927, are Quebec Premier Louis-Alexandre Taschereau, Prime Minister Mackenzie King and Ontario Premier Howard Ferguson.   *(Public Archives Canada)*

of frequent disputes and discords between the two levels of government. That is a constant of our history, as it probably is of most federations.

Rather than go into any detail, I will start, as the joint committee did itself, with the Balfour Declaration[24] of 1926, which, you will recall, set Canada on its path to full nationhood.

Essentially, one thing was missing for Canada to achieve that status. Through no fault of the British government, but because it was a self-imposed obstacle, Canada had not agreed on an amending formula which would permit it to bring back the Constitution and so to have a constitution of its own. Therefore, in 1927, the year after the Balfour Declaration, Mackenzie King convened a federal-provincial conference — Dominion-provincial conference, as they were then called — and asked the provinces to try to agree on an amending formula.

I will not read the whole story, of course. I will only read from Professor McNaught's *History of Canada*, at page 246:

> The decade's surge of provincialism was symbolized by a Dominion-Provincial Conference in 1927 at which the Tory Premier Ferguson of Ontario and Liberal Premier Taschereau of Québec joined in proclaiming the ''compact theory'' of Confederation — a position which would give near autonomy to the provinces and which saw federal powers as being merely delegated to Ottawa by the provinces.

Naturally the Compact theory caused the conference to end in failure. Exactly 60 years and eight prime ministers would pass into history before the provinces were able to find a prime minister of Canada who was prepared to capitulate to that view of Confederation, that is, a compact between the provinces to set up a federal government.

I intend discussing that today. But before I do I want to say that during those 60 years federal governments were very

Canada's 13th prime minister, John Diefenbaker, with Canadian Bill of Rights documentation, September 5, 1958. This human rights charter, which was passed in 1960, applied to federal, not provincial law, since provincial consent was not obtained. *(D. Cameron; Public Archives Canada)*

active in trying to create a national will, a sense of national identity which would lead Canadians to believe that Canada was more than the sum of the wills of the provinces, but that it had a will of its own — "une volonté générale," as Rousseau had called it, or "un vouloir-vivre collectif" in more conventional terms. There is some national will which is more than the sum total of the provincial wills.

Various prime ministers attempted in various ways to create a body of values to be shared by the Canadian people. Mackenzie King did it by establishing a network of social security[25] which would bind the people together. Mr. St. Laurent, you will recall, did it, first, by amending section 91, or having the British Parliament amend it,[26] so that Canada, at least in things which did not involve the provinces and language and education, could amend its Constitution. Mr. St. Laurent also, of course, stopped the appeal to the Privy Council so that we had a supreme judicial tribunal of our own.[27]

Mr. Diefenbaker brought in the Bill of Rights.[28] He was unable to constitutionalize it, because his minister, Mr. Fulton, had not been able to get the provinces to agree to a formula for amending. Therefore, Mr. Diefenbaker's Bill of Rights, which was certainly a nomenclature of values which bound Canadians together in the sense that they all shared certain basic beliefs, was never put into the Constitution, though it remains as an important stepping stone.

Bilingualism Unites People; Dualism Divides Them

Mr. Pearson attempted, with the B and B Commission,[29] to seek ways in which the dissatisfaction of the French-speaking people in Canada — and, to a certain extent, some ethnic groups — could be met in a way which would not divide Canada, which would not create dualism, which, as we shall see later, is what the 1987 accord does. Dualism, by definition, is a division of people. Mr. Pearson was proposing bilingualism, which is a quality of individuals or institutions which tends to unite them rather than separate them.

Finally, one of the more recent prime ministers (Mr. Trudeau) brought in a Charter of Rights and Freedoms entrenched in the Constitution, and which was meant to create a body of values and beliefs that not only united all Canadians in feeling that they were one nation, but also set them above the governments of the provinces and the federal government itself. Thus the people have rights which no legislative body can abridge, therefore establishing the sovereignty of the Canadian people over all institutions of government.

But all Canadian prime ministers failed in their attempts to assert the national will by patriating the Constitution. The reason is very simple to explain. Every attempt was predicated on the idea that patriation and an amending formula — and, even more, a Charter — could only proceed with unanimous consent, that is, the consent of each and every province. So there was no national will possible beyond that defined by the 11 First Ministers. Of course, that permitted every province to hold the country to ransom by saying, ''Well, I will agree to patriation which is, perhaps, good for the Canadian people. It's the way to express ourselves as a nation. But I will only do it if you give me some rights in exchange.'' I do not like to use the word ''blackmail,'' but certainly there was a process of ''leverage'' being used with the result that Canada could only exist as a full and complete nation by leave, not of its people, but by leave of each and every one of the ten premiers.

The story goes on and time goes by, which it does in this place also. I have figures from National Accounts-Income and Expenditures, July 1965, table 37. There was a period in the early 1950s to the middle 1960s where there was an extraordinary amount of growth in the provinces for reasons which everyone knows — new areas of legislation were coming into

E. Davie Fulton, former minister of justice and co-creator of the
Fulton-Favreau formula, on Parliament Hill, 1966.   *(Canadian Press)*

Prime Minister Pierre Trudeau, Quebec Premier Robert Bourassa, and Louis Robichaud, premier of New Brunswick (1960–70), at the September 1970 Federal-Provincial Conference, Ottawa. *(Public Archives Canada)*

play, and the provinces saw that it was within their jurisdiction. They were acting to replace the private concept of schools and hospitals. There was a complete reversal of the proportion between federal and provincial spending. From 60/40 federal-provincial, it had gone to 40/60 federal-provincial during those years. The provinces were not only spending a lot and taxing a lot, although some of it was by way of tax points given to the provinces by the federal government. The provincial governments grew proudly; they developed expertise; they had competent bureaucracies; and they felt they could manage their own affairs and also manage all of the affairs that, until then, had been managed by the federal government.

This was just a continuation of the tensions which, I recalled, had begun in John A. Macdonald's day: a struggle for power, a struggle for money, and generally a struggle for both between the two levels of government.

Eventually, a whole new operation was put into place. The provinces began acting collectively to force the federal government to transfer powers to them in exchange for their consent to patriation. We start with the Fulton-Favreau formula of 1964.[30] The repatriation process came unstuck, because Premier Lesage and his principal minister, René Lévesque in those days, both backed out of an agreement that they had not only agreed to but had also begun to defend publicly. They were made to understand that they might have a good amending formula, but they had not won more powers for Quebec in the process and, therefore, they backed out.

Two years later Premier Daniel Johnson,[31] whose slogan was ''Equality or Independence!'' — equality between the two nations or independence of one from the other — was demanding all the powers needed to safeguard Quebec's identity in preparation for what was to be Premier Robarts'[32] Confederation For Tomorrow Conference, held in Toronto in 1967.[33]

It then came to June 1971, when Premier Bourassa withdrew from the patriation agreement that he had proposed[34] — an amending formula that he had put forward, plus a lot of other powers for the provinces, including some role in the nomination of judges, and so on. He claimed that in exchange for his signature, he should get "something of substance" in the social area. In concrete terms, that meant, for instance, that in Family Allowances the federal government would hand the money to the provinces who in turn would pay them out, courtesy of the provincial government, in a way which might vary for socio-economic reasons from province to province. The minister, Marc Lalonde, had worked out an administrative arrangement whereby that might be done without actually transferring power and money, just permitting the province to decide how it should be distributed. That worked well, but it was not a constitutional amendment, and therefore it was not enough.

We will hear the same story later on when we come to immigration agreements. It is not enough that the provinces get to manage the federal government's affairs; they want it to be put into the Constitution so that the federal government actually gives up its power forever rather than just signing an administrative arrangement.

Every Other Premier Had Caught On

By 1976 Mr. Bourassa had added cultural sovereignty to his demands for Quebec; but by then every other premier had caught on, because every premier realized that his consent was needed to patriate the Constitution. Therefore, he would trade his consent for as much power as he could get in whatever area he thought was important for his province. In other words, each province was in a position to exact its own price for permitting the Canadian people to have a Constitution of their own.

So that I am not talking too abstractly, at this point I will read the provincial demands put together at the interprovincial conference in the summer of 1976, chaired by Premier

Lougheed. You will see a familiar number of items in this particular list, which dates back to 1976. It covered the following areas: immigration (dealt with in 1987); language rights (dealt with in 1982); resource taxation (dealt with in 1982); the federal declaratory power — that is section 92(10)(c) of the Constitution, which would be amended to require provincial consent; annual conference of First Ministers (dealt with in the 1987 accord); creation of new provinces — we get that in the 1987 accord, too; culture, which really was saying provincial paramountcy in culture and all the arts, literature and cultural heritage. That was dealt with also in 1987. Then there was communications. I will read you some speeches later on from Mr. Bourassa and Mr. Rémillard, saying that in culture and communications they feel they have achieved what they want with the "distinct society" clause. The Supreme Court of Canada was included in the 1976 list; the federal spending power — also in the 1976 list; and regional equalization, which we had dealt with in the 1982 accord.

You can say one thing for the provinces: They are bloody consistent! I do not mind saying, as a Quebecer, that Quebec's hand is clearly seen behind all of this. That was the story of 1976.

Let us now go to the summer of 1978. The interprovincial conference was chaired this time by Premier Blakeney, of the NDP. The 1976 conference was chaired by a Conservative; this one was chaired by a Social Democrat, but he had been joined by a Separatist, Premier Lévesque. As he came to the conference, Lévesque made a declaration. The Quebec declaration said that, while committed to its option of sovereignty association, it could generally go along with the 1976 consensus and most of the other constitutional points raised in Regina. We will come to those. Quebec went on to state that "this approach falls within the mandate of the Quebec government to reinforce provincial rights within the present system and also illustrates some of the minimal changes required to make the federal system a serious alternative in

The two constitutional rivals, Pierre Trudeau and René Lévesque, during a federal-provincial conference. *(Canadian Press)*

the forthcoming Quebec referendum'' — forthcoming, but some four years later.

What were these "minimal changes"? Here is the 1978 consensus: "In addition to the 1976 list" — that I have just given to you — "the premiers, in the course of their discussion in Regina, have reached agreement on a number of additional substantive matters on which federal views are invited.

"First, abolition of the now obsolete federal powers to reserve or disallow provincial legislation."

Well, obsolete, but maybe some people sitting in Ottawa some day will be glad that they are still in the Constitution Act, because disallowance of some provincial acts may some day remain as the only way to avoid the destruction of the federal government.

"Second, a clear limitation on the federal power to implement treaties so that it cannot be used to invade areas of provincial jurisdiction." We are hearing about that nowadays.

"Third, the establishment of an appropriate provincial jurisdiction with respect to fisheries." Well, we have that on the agenda of the next conferences.

"Fourth, confirmation and strengthening of provincial powers with respect to natural resources." That was done in 1982, and, incidentally, for those who say that the provinces got nothing out of 1982 — and I will come back to that later — quite a bit of power was transferred from the federal government to the provinces by the November 1981 accord, which became the Constitution Act of 1982.

"Fifth, full and formal consultation with the provinces in appointments to the superior, district and county courts of the provinces." That would be the next step.

"Sixth, appropriate provincial involvement in appointments to the Supreme Court of Canada." This is a modest agenda, as you will see.

"Further, there was a consensus that a number of additional matters require early consideration: the federal emergency power; the federal residual power dealing with peace, order and good government; the formal access of the provinces to the field of indirect taxation; amending formula and patriation; and the delegation of legislative powers between governments. All premiers expressed grave concern that section 109, concerning provincial ownership of natural resources, had not been carried forward into the proposed new Constitution.''

So, after this modest beginning in 1976 and 1978, eventually we reach September 1980.

What happened in September/October of 1980? By that time it had become obvious that the greed of the provinces was a bottomless pit, and that the price to be paid to the provinces for their consent to patriation with some kind of an entrenched Charter — which had been requested as far back as 1971 in Victoria — was nothing less than acceptance by the federal government of the ''compact'' theory, which would transform Canada from a very decentralized, yet balanced federation, into some kind of a loose confederation. That is when our government said, ''Enough. We are going to move unilaterally and we are going to give the people their Constitution and their Charter of Rights. You can like it or lump it, but this is what we intend to do,'' and honourable senators know the rest of the story: The matter went to the courts — and I will come to that in a moment.

Quite frankly, the reason we were determined, and almost desperate, to move without paying this enormous price that the provinces had asked of us in September of 1980 was that we had promised renewal of the Constitution when we were fighting the referendum. At that time we had said we would put our seats at stake that we would bring renewal. I will come to that in a moment.

Blackmail Unlimited

But first, honourable senators, let me just read the somewhat immodest agenda that was put before the federal government in September of 1980 by all of the provinces. Quebec had made a proposal and it became a common stand of the provinces. It was discussed by the provincial ministers on September 11, and then by the premiers at breakfast on September 12; it was then brought over to the Prime Minister of Canada the same day, and here is what the Prime Minister of Canada was told would need to be done to the Constitution if we were to proceed some day with patriation:

> The provinces of Canada unanimously agree in principle to the following changes to be made to the Constitution of Canada. It is understood that these changes are to be considered as a global package and that this agreement is a common effort to come to a significant first step towards a thorough renewal of the Canadian federation.

I do not intend to read all of the details of it, but on the list there is natural resources; communications; Upper Chamber; Supreme Court of Canada; judicature, which repeals section 96 which permits the federal government to appoint judges of superior and provincial courts; family law; fisheries; offshore resources; equalization. Then we come to item 9, "a Charter of Rights"; but the Charter would have to be brought in with a *non obstante* clause, and with a clause that all existing laws would be deemed valid. In other words, a "Charter" which was grandfathering government rights over the people.

Under item 10, we would get patriation, but with the Alberta amending formula, which, in the event, was the one that we ended up with.[35] Item 11: powers over the economy; item 12: a preamble. The latter is a Quebec proposal, which I might take time to read to you, but you would not like it.

The document that I was handed at that time (and which became known as the Chateau Consensus) goes on to say:

> If a satisfactory interprovincial consensus is reached in this way, it must be accompanied, when tabled, by announcement of the following measures:

As soon as the federal government has given its assent to this consensus, the matter will be returned to the ministers for drafting;

Another list of subjects must be established to be covered by the constitutional discussions at the ministerial level in the following months. These subjects are: The horizontal powers of the federal government — spending power; declaratory power; power to act for peace, order and good government — culture; social affairs; urban and regional affairs; regional development; transportation policy; international affairs; the administration of justice . . .

And so on. I do not think history will blame us for having said, "Enough; we are not going to trade all of these things just so that the people of Canada can be sovereign in their own land." After all, we had won the 1980 referendum by making a promise of renewal, and it had become obvious that the rule of provincial unanimity, particularly with a Separatist premier heading the government of Quebec, would continue to render impossible the first step towards renewal (i.e. repatriation), as it had, indeed, without interruption since the 1927 conference.

Therefore, in a sense, we were in a Catch 22 situation. The federal government was told that it must renew the Constitution, and that had begun with Premier Robarts' meeting in 1967. Therefore, the federal Government of Canada must renew the Constitution, but, on the other hand, they must be prevented from renewing the Constitution until the federal government gave the provinces all the power they were asking for. In other words, for the provinces, the renewing of the Constitution could only mean one thing: transferring more powers to the provinces. The people of Canada could not have their own Constitution until their national government accepted its own dismemberment!

There is an allegation that is frequently made not only by Quebec nationalists but by more serious people such as academics. It was also made by the Prime Minister of Canada; it was made by Senator Murray in an article that he sent to *La Presse* and to the *Globe and Mail* on June 15. Let me read it:

> The solemn promise made to Quebecers during the referendum that federalism would be renewed and the Constitution amended to reflect the *distinct identity* and aspirations of Quebec was unfortunately not kept.

Mr. Mulroney said the same thing on October 21 of last year, which is quoted in *Hansard*. At that time he said that the federal forces — and I know whom he means — had promised that we would renew the confederation, and, in order to prove our good faith as reformers, the allegation is made that we would have had to bring in renewal of a kind that would carry the assent of the very premier, Mr. Lévesque, who was bent on taking his province out of Canada.

If the absurdity of the circular reasoning contained in that proposition is not obvious, let me state it otherwise: I had been writing, speaking and publishing for some 20 years against any form of special status, such as two nations or the two-Canada concept. Of course, I never said that I would renew federalism by giving Mr. Lévesque what he wanted and by giving the provinces what they asked for in this enormous list of September 1980. I said we would renew the federation, and anyone who had listened to my campaign speeches or the debates on federal/provincial affairs could not possibly assume and, in turn, write in good faith that we had promised to give Quebec some form of "distinct society."

Honourable senators, how could it reasonably be inferred that I was attempting to win the referendum by setting Canada on a course that I had consistently denounced as deleterious to the integrity of Canada; as deleterious as even losing the referendum itself would be? I really take objection to not only Senator Murray but to the Prime Minister and the devil of a lot of academics implying that, somehow, we had made promises to give the Province of Quebec, in a reformed Constitution, what the Separatists and some ultra nationalists were asking. There was no point in winning the referendum if we were going to give to those who had lost it everything they were trying to get by winning it.

We proceeded unilaterally and the resolution we introduced on October 10, 1980, contained none of the flaws which Senator Murray says "tainted" the November 1981 agreement with the provinces. There was no opting out; there was no notwithstanding clause; and, of course, Quebec would have been in on the same basis as every other province. I have here the October 2 proposed resolution for a joint address, but, of course, I will not read it. However, let me point out two things. Sections 1 to 30 set people above governments. The people were getting a Charter with no notwithstanding clause in it. That was the first step in our history to recognize the sovereignty of the people. But, through the amending procedure, it was done even more clearly, because what it says in this resolution is that if we cannot get unanimity on an amending formula — we were hoping it would be the Victoria formula — then we would ask the people to decide what amending formula they wanted. We would give them a choice. Either the people would vote for an amending formula put forward by the provinces — and to make it a serious one there had to be eight provinces to agree on an amending formula, and there was a "gang of eight"[36] which was developing, so it was not a figure taken out of thin air — or an amending formula put forward by the federal government which, in our view, was going to be the Victoria formula — it says so in the resolution. However, it could have been changed as a result of negotiations. The people would have had a clear choice.

This was recognizing the sovereignty of the people over the fundamental act of the Constitution, but, better still, we had a section 42, which also set up a referendum process in a free-standing way so that at any time, if there were a deadlock in Canada, the people, as in most democratic countries, could be called upon to express their views. That is what we put before the people and the Parliaments in October of 1980.

You will remember what happened. Three provinces asked for a reference to the Supreme Court,[37] saying that we could not proceed unilaterally. A lot of Indians and premiers went and had dinner in London. There was a House of Lords committee saying that we were very nasty, but, until the Supreme Court judgment in the middle of spring, we were doing what seemed, at least to me, what circumstances had forced us to do after 54 years, that is, from 1927 to 1981.

If Canada could not give itself a constitution of its own, perhaps we should ask Britain to give it to us. Margaret Thatcher, God bless her — I do not say that on everything — told me, "If the Canadian Parliament asks me for something and it has a majority supporting a resolution, there is nothing much I can do to prevent it." I think the Britons had in mind — and, I think, wisely — the principle of "no independence without majority rule" in Rhodesia, which became Zimbabwe.

However, the courts decided otherwise; they decided that what we were doing was legal, but, you will recall, they decided it was not conventional by virtue of a convention which was so uncertain and obscure that they could not define it. They knew that consent did not have to be of all provinces, but they knew that, somehow, two provinces were not enough. However, they did not know how many in between. That was a vague convention, to say the least. They said our resolution was legal, but it was not nice. Since I was known to be a person who liked to do things nicely, I met with the provinces again and we hammered out the November 5, 1981, agreement. It had other flaws. I note that Professor Tony Hall was before you recently saying that aboriginal rights had been left out in the bargaining with the provinces. I could add, too, that women's rights had been left out, not in our draft

Prime Minister Pierre Trudeau listens expressionlessly as Quebec Premier René Lévesque denounces the constitutional agreement worked out at the November 1981 Federal-Provincial Conference. *(Canadian Press)*

of September, 1980, but in the negotiations with the provinces. Two of them wanted Indians and women excluded, so, in order to get our Constitution and the rest of the Charter, we took them out.

They, too, were put back in after the signature of November 5, and that is why I return to the Meech Lake and Langevin Block agreement. Everybody but Mr. Lévesque had signed that original accord on November 5, 1981, but, still, we were able to improve it to include women and the aboriginals. Something like that happened between Meech Lake and the Langevin Block.[38] If that could happen, one wonders why other amendments, which were necessary, could not have been brought in.

I think it is important to say here that the November 5, 1981 agreement, which became the Constitution Act, 1982, gave a lot of new powers to the provinces, including Quebec. Apart from the Charter and patriation which the people of Canada were getting, that agreement of 1981 was based essentially on the Alberta amending formula and on various agendas that I read to you which did several things to transfer powers to the provinces.

Remember that the November 1981 accord did not give any power to the federal government. In a sense, it limited the power of all governments, federal and provincial, by a Charter, but it actually transferred a lot of power from the federal government to the provincial governments. It did so in the area of natural resources, giving the provinces the power of indirect taxation and the power of external trade. It entrenched equalization payments. These are things that Quebec had been asking for since 1976 and beyond. I am sure you will remember the list I read to you. It included more power over natural resources, equalization and the right to opt out of certain constitutional amendments, which I had not offered in the Victoria formula, but which the provinces demanded. Well, they got it. They got the right to opt out of certain constitutional amendments, which was something that, until then, they had not had under the British North America Act.

More important still, under section 41, they gained the right of a constitutional veto that no province alone had until then. Every province can stop the federal government and a national consensus from achieving reform in certain defined areas. Until then, under section 91, the federal government could, at least, amend all those things.

There was a vast amount of new power given to the provinces from the list drawn up by the "gang of eight," of which Quebec was one of the more notorious members, so, to those who say that Quebec got nothing I would point out that although they did not say, "Thank you," they still got a lot.

I can come back to that, but I know that time goes on. That is how we get to Quebec's five demands. They had not got *everything* in November of 1981. Quebec came up with five demands, and that was called the "Quebec Round."[39] Mind you, on every one of those demands the federal government had offered some concessions in the past, during the 1968-1980 negotiations. Therefore, I completely understand Premier Bourassa saying, "Well, this is our package. We were offered something before. We got a lot in 1981, but we would like some more, since you offered it in the past. Let's get it now." The situation was different from our point of view, because we had offered a lot, bargaining to get a Charter of Rights in the Constitution. But in 1987, Quebec was not offering anything in exchange that I know of, but it was bargaining for more powers in five more areas.

Quebec's Five Demands

I want to examine them in detail, because frequent allegations have been made that the 1987 process flowed naturally out of the 1968-80 negotiations. I have the quotes of Mr. Mulroney, Senator Tremblay and practically all of the members of the joint committee of the Senate and the House of

Commons. I have all of these quotes, which I can get into, but they all say, "Well, after all, the Trudeau government had offered all of these things. What is the big fuss, that they are objecting now to the fact that we are giving them at Meech Lake and in the Langevin Block?"

I want to go into some detail with each one of these five demands to show that the way they were met in 1987 brought Canada in a diametrically opposite direction to the way in which Canada would have gone in each of the other cases. In other words, when, between 1968 and 1980, we were offering certain concessions to the provinces, it was always in a way which was not destructive of the national will, of the reality that there was a Canadian "vouloir-vivre collectif" which would bind everyone, even if everyone and his brother had not said, "Yes, okay." In other words, we were never conceding that unanimity would have to prevail.

Quebec's First Demand

I will take the demands in turn. I will start with the veto on constitutional amendments. Well, of course, before Meech Lake there was no veto for Quebec; and the Supreme Court made that quite clear [40] — when the matter was brought before it in 1982 — that there never had been a veto for Quebec or for anyone else. There was some kind of convention, that you needed more than a couple of provinces, but none had an absolute veto.

We offered a veto to Quebec in the Victoria Charter. [41] It was a formula — I will not go into details again — which essentially called for the federal government and six provinces. Quebec had a veto, and everyone agreed, except Quebec! But Quebec had proposed it. It was Quebec and five provinces; but the idea of a national will was defined at least in a way which did not permit every province to exercise some form of blackmail.

We offered that formula throughout the 1970s, including in the October 10, 1980, draft. But it was rejected by

The eight dissenting premiers who disagreed with Prime Minister
Trudeau's constitutional package, at breakfast, November 1981.
Clockwise from left: Brian Peckford, Newfoundland, Allan
Blakeney, Saskatchewan, Angus MacLean, Prince Edward Island,
John Buchanan, Nova Scotia, Réne Lévesque, Quebec, Peter
Lougheed, Alberta, William Bennett, British Columbia and Sterling
Lyon of Manitoba, back to camera.   *(Canadian Press)*

Premier Bourassa in 1971, and it was rejected by Premier Lévesque and the "gang of eight" in 1980 and 1981. What Quebec was asking for was something that had been offered to them. But they did not want it. Why? Because as soon as they had said, "Yes" to something, then we would have had a Constitution and they would not be able to use their leverage to get more.

I take exception to Senator Murray's saying that I proposed unanimous consent on March 31, 1976. Senator Murray, in his testimony on August 4, at page 286 of the proceedings, said:

I should note that applying unanimity to this narrow range —

He is talking about section 41:

— is much more modest than the March 31, 1976 proposal of Prime Minister Trudeau, which would have required unanimous consent for all major amendments.

I never proposed that. Senator Murray or his people misread the letter that on March 31, 1976, I sent to Premier Lougheed, with a copy to all premiers. I will not read it all. It comprises several pages. Let me sum it up, and I challenge Senator Murray to contradict it tomorrow — if someone wants to work all night to look that up.

What I suggested was three methods of getting patriation with an amending formula. One called for unanimous consent, in which I say, "This approach would introduce a rigidity which does not now exist." Then I suggested two other methods: "The second and preferable alternative would be . . ."and so on. Then I said that "A third and more extensive possibility would be to include . . ." and so on. So there are three possibilities there. I sum it up by saying:

As you can see, in my letter to Premier Lougheed, there are several possibilities as to the course of action now to take. So far this is clear. So far as the federal government is concerned —

My preference:

> — our much preferred course would be to act in unison with all of the provinces. Patriation is such an historic milestone and it would be better if we could get unison.

I read on:

> But if unanimity does not appear possible, the federal government will have to decide whether it will recommend to Parliament that a joint address be passed seeking patriation.

What I am saying, in essence, is that we would like unanimity to patriate the Constitution with an amending formula, and we are prepared to wait for unanimity to get it back with an amending formula; but the amending formula itself will not call for unanimity.

So, for Senator Murray to say that Trudeau's proposal would have required unanimous consent for all major amendments is wrong. I was still saying in 1976 that we need to get everyone in in order to get it back from Great Britain. But, once it is back, no unanimity rule; the Victoria rule.

With Meech Lake there is no national will left. Any province can opt out of a constitutional amendment transferring power to the federal government and get full compensation.[42] So a province can opt out in the matter of powers. But then, more importantly, under the new section 41, any province has a veto; any province can prevent a constitutional amendment wanted by nine other provinces and the federal government on all federal institutions of government — the Senate,

he House of Commons, the Supreme Court and the Terri-
ories.

When you remember that some of the western provinces
are not, shall we say, all that cooperative with the desire of
natives to achieve some of the aboriginal and native rights,
t is, I think, wrong to have given each province the right
o prevent the Government of Canada — and perhaps six
or seven other provinces — from exercising the right to agree,
for instance, that the Territories should be established into
provinces so that in some way the place where the majority
of the native people live could achieve some form of self-
government, as the provinces themselves had.

So that is why I say that with Meech Lake, on the first Quebec demand, the solution was not like our solution, which
respected the idea of a national will binding all; but it was
a solution which destroyed the existence of a national will
and submitted it to the unanimous consent of every province.

Quebec's Second Demand

The second Quebec demand was on limitation of the federal spending power. Before Meech Lake we had made a
proposal in June of 1969[43] which, once again, was predicated
on the existence of a national will, and we defined it then
as ''an affirmative vote in a majority of senatorial divisions,''
which in effect meant that five to seven provinces plus the
federal government could establish a shared-cost program in
areas of provincial jurisdiction.

Under that proposal, if a premier did not want to go along,
he was not forced to go along, but, rather than have compensation paid into the provincial treasury, as we have in the
Langevin formula, the federal government would give the
money back to the people (by a form of negative taxation)
so that provincial popular sovereignty would be respected in
the sense that the people of a province would not be penal-
ized because their premier wanted to thwart the national will.

That is a lot different from what came out of Meech Lake, where there is no effort to seek to establish a national will. On the contrary, there is encouragement given to provinces that want to opt out of national programs by compensation, providing the province carried on "a program or initiative that is compatible with the national objective." Who sets national objectives? Is it Parliament, or is it the 11 First Ministers? That is something that should be clarified before the members vote on this. And what does "compatible" mean? Is it something which is not a complete denial of the federal program, or what?

Quebec's Third Demand

The third Quebec demand was a provincial role in appointments to the Supreme Court of Canada. Before Meech Lake, the BNA Act, of course, in section 101, stated that all aspects of the Supreme Court were under the jurisdiction of Parliament.

In the 1971 Victoria Charter, article 27 provided for, as Quebec was asking in its third demand, a provincial role in appointments to the Supreme Court of Canada. That was worked out with Quebec and the other provinces and it had been agreed to. What was the formula? It was that the Attorney General of Canada would always consult with the attorney general of the province from where he proposed to appoint someone to the Supreme Court of Canada. If there was no agreement, the Attorney General of Canada would set up an electoral college, appointed in agreement by both sides, and chaired by someone, if they could not agree, appointed by the Chief Justice of Canada. So there was a proposal for an electoral college to which the federal government would submit three names that had been tested with the province, and that college would choose one.

This was provincial involvement; it might not have been enough, maybe it was too much, but, at any rate, it was provincial involvement of a kind that had been accepted by the ten provinces at Victoria. What we proposed in Bill C-60 in 1978 repeated somewhat the same scheme.

What is in Meech Lake? The federal government gives up its absolute power under section 101 of the BNA Act by having to select judges exclusively from a provincial list. The Meech Lake Accord, in section 101C. (1) — and I am sure you have all read it again and again — states that the government of each province "may" submit names, and the federal government "shall" appoint a person whose name has been submitted. That is what I call remote control of the Supreme Court by the provinces. But it may mortally wound the Supreme Court because of the not unheard of proposition where a province wants to break up Canada and be a spoiler. It says the province "may" submit names, but what if it does not? Is there some emergency power that will permit us to "go around" the Constitution and fill the vacancies on the Supreme Court anyhow? Or does it mean that, for instance, in the example I have in mind, if Premier Lévesque were operating under this dispensation, and we were to end up with only six out of nine Supreme Court judges, all named by the "Anglos", with many judicial cases coming from Quebec — and they would be judged fairly, I am sure — but to the extent that the judgments were not favourable to the Quebec government, you can imagine the kind of mess it would make, apart from the fact it is doubtful whether the court could operate legally if it had, over a long period of time, only six out of nine judges sitting. So there is no provision for breaking that kind of log-jam.

As you know — and I will not go into it, because it is not one of Quebec's five demands — the same applies to the Senate. Some of us in this place — if I can say I am in this place, at least, for this afternoon — were in the House of Commons when one man, Gilles Grégoire[44], was able to cause a devil of a lot of obstruction by refusing unanimous consent on a lot of things. He really slowed down the work of Parliament. So what would it be if a province sent up twenty-four or six or ten senators? It would be something like when the Irish Home Rulers disrupted the work of the British Parliament.

So I do not think it is a satisfactory way of respecting or establishing the national will. Certainly it is not fair to say that since I had proposed something quite different on the Supreme Court, I should not object to this particular way of appointing judges. That is like saying: You do not mind if something is white so why do you object if something is black?

Quebec's Fourth Demand

The fourth demand of Quebec was a greater provincial role in immigration. Before Meech Lake, section 95 of the BNA Act said that Parliament may make laws in relation to immigration with all and any of the provinces, and provincial laws shall have effect only as far as they are not repugnant to any Act of the Parliament of Canada.

But we recognized that the provinces, though in a subordinate position, had particular demands as to what kind of immigrants they would need for work purposes or language purposes, so we made contractual arrangements. We made them with Quebec, and we made them with other provinces. Otto Lang began in 1971, Robert Andras in 1975, and Bud Cullen in 1978.[45] They were agreements, which were renegotiated from time to time to meet different circumstances, but there was no transfer of constitutional power. In fact, because they were contracts they could be changed and renegotiated, but an immigrant who comes to a province is also an immigrant who comes to Canada. You don't cease to come to Canada just because you are going to a province. Most immigrants come to a province because they want to be Canadians.

Therefore, our contracts were in respect of the national will of Canadians.

What do we have with Meech Lake? Well, the federal government gives up much of its paramountcy, and it gives it up irreversibly. Once a contract has been signed it will be onstitutionalized, so the accord says, and it can only be hanged by using the constitutional amending formula, which means that any province can prevent an accord which is favourable to it from being amended in the slightest way.

There are some funny provisions in there, but I will not go into them in detail. There is a guarantee in the Langevin Block agreement that Quebec will be guaranteed a share of immigrants proportionate to its share of the total population of Canada. What happens if people don't want to go to Quebec? Presumably, that means the other provinces cannot take the immigrants they want, because they will be diluting Quebec's share, but also, Quebec has a right to have 5 per cent more, and similar agreements may be signed with all other provinces. How you can guarantee 5 per cent more to all of the provinces is something I cannot work out.

These are silly things drafted in haste, and the people were told that they could not ever change them no matter how silly they were, because the whole thing might fall apart.

The most offensive clause is the one that says Canada will withdraw services for the reception and integration, including linguistic and cultural, of all foreign nationals wishing to settle in Quebec. With reasonable compensation to be paid to the province for doing Canada's job!

Well, we are all grown-ups. I do not have to make many drawings to get you to understand that if you have government and immigration officials who are determined to make sure that everybody coming into Canada has a conception of Canada as being a pact between provinces, as being a country where only French should be spoken in one province and only English in all of the others, you could have a situation where the national will is thwarted. I keep coming back to the same expression, because I have to answer those who say: "Well, I proposed something on immigration in Cullen-Couture, therefore, why am I objecting to this particular proposal in the Constitutional Accord?" It is completely different, because once the provinces have gotten into that area of reception and integration of all foreign nationals, and

Sir George-Etienne Cartier in 1867. One of the Fathers of
Confederation, he was the dominant figure in Quebec politics for a
generation.   *(Wm. Notman & Son, Montreal; National Archives of
Canada)*

are being paid to get into that area, they are not going to get out even if the federal government says, ''Tut, tut, tut, now, you are not teaching the love of Canada to these people, you are teaching the love of western alienation, or whatever it is.''

Once again, I think that if immigrants are going to be taught the theory of provincial sovereignty, it will not make for a strong Canada. We are having trouble enough now trying to build a nation with common values without starting to provincialize immigrants. We can already work on children, since children are under provincial jurisdiction in schools. But are we now to start to work on immigrants so that they have a conception of Canada which corresponds to that which the provinces defined in the Chateau consensus of September 1980? I repeat that an immigrant to a province is an immigrant to Canada, and that Canada has no moral right to give up its jurisdiction in that area.

Quebec's Fifth Demand: A Distinct Society

Finally, to the recognition of Quebec as a distinct society. It is a tough one to tackle. But, in essence, what is federalism? It is a form of government where the exercise of sovereignty is divided between two levels of government so that each can legislate, tax and spend in areas of its jurisdiction concerning people within its territory. That is what federalism is. When the Fathers of Confederation discussed the BNA Act in 1867, that is what they had in mind. They gave to the provinces all of the powers outlined under section 92, which were, as jurisprudence tells us, generously interpreted by the Privy Council and by the Law Lords in favour of provincial rights.[46] They gave all of this to the provinces so that they could develop as distinct societies. So what is the big deal?

Of course Quebec is a distinct society with its own language and its civil law, which it has a right to have under section

Jean Lesage (centre), premier of Quebec from 1960 to 1966, father of the Quiet Revolution, promoter of the special status vaguely defined but summarized in the slogan "Maîtres chez nous." Here he is with economist Eric Kierans, later to be postmaster general, then minister of communications in the Trudeau Cabinet, at the Quebec Liberal Party Convention in October 1967. *(Canada Wide Picture Service; Public Archives Canada)*

92.13. Of course it became even more distinct with the "quiet revolution," when Premier Lesage began to use the organs of a modern state to mould that society as a distinct one. And of course it became even more distinct when a Separatist premier was elected and tried to move the people of that province and that society in a completely different direction. It is a distinct society, and nobody is denying that. Nobody would probably even deny that, if you want, we can put it into a preamble somewhere. That might cause some pique with the Newfoundlanders, though, who only came into Canada in the lifetime of most of the people in this room. They could certainly say, "Well, why not us? Newfoundland and Labrador are a distinct society." There might be some dissatisfaction, but, at least, it would be doubtful that any legal confusion would arise. So you have distinct societies, some more distinct than others. I agree, if you like, that I am more distinct than Senator Marchand here — no, no, that's not right, he was distinct before I was!

All right, we are all distinct. But particularly after constitutionalists have been discussing preambles for a long period of time, when you deliberately do not put "distinct society" into a preamble but put it into an interpretative clause, that can mean only one thing — you are giving to the government of that distinct society powers that it did not have before. If you are entrenching the distinctiveness as a special provision, you can only be doing it because you want to give special powers. That is why every time Quebec asked our government for special status or the recognition of its distinct society or sovereignty association, we would resist. It was not a fight for the distinctiveness of the Canadian people — they had that. It could only be a fight for more power for the provincial politicians. Yet Quebec's distinctiveness, I am proud to say, was probably served as well, if not better, through organs of culture like Radio Canada, the CBC, the Film Board and the Arts Council, all creations of the *federal* government, who rewarded quality of production, quality of

Claude Ryan, outstanding journalist with *Le Devoir*, which he ran between 1964 and 1978. Subsequently leader of the Quebec Liberal Party, he was René Lévesque's adversary in the 1980 Referendum campaign. In January 1980, Ryan issued a document on constitutional reform known as the "Beige Paper" which sided with the federalist option in that a new constitution would confer upon Quebec a "special status" characterized by vastly increased powers.   *(Canadian Press)*

French and quality of artistry, which was not always found in Quebec institutions.

So why not put distinctiveness in a preamble? If that is what you want, you can encapsulate it there. We had drafted several preambles, one in Bill C-60, which I will not bother reading to you. There was one drafted in June 1980, which I will bother reading to you, but I will not get far, you will see. I see that the first I mentioned was not in Bill C-60 — it was in the prologue to Bill C-60. On June 10, 1980, which can be found in the House of Commons *Hansard* at page 1977, I was tabling in the House of Commons an appendix. I suggested an agenda for a meeting of the First Ministers on the Constitution. This reads:

A STATEMENT OF PRINCIPLES FOR A NEW CONSTITUTION

We, the people of Canada —
I do not have time to read it all, but I wish I did, because it was not bad prose. It was panned by the press and by the premiers, but it is a good preamble.

> We, the people of Canada, proudly proclaim that we are and shall always be, with the help of God, a free and self-governing people.
>
> Born of a meeting of the English and French presence on North American soil which had long been the home of our native peoples, and enriched by the contribution of millions of people from the four corners of the earth, we have chosen to create a life together which transcends the differences of blood relationships, language and religion, and willingly accept the experience of sharing our wealth and cultures, while respecting our diversity.
>
> We have chosen to live together in one sovereign country, a true federation, conceived as a constitutional monarchy and founded on democratic principles.
>
> Faithful to our history . . .

I think it was pretty hard to beat, but, look it was panned by the English-speaking columnists, and do you want to know what happened in Quebec? It did not get beyond the fifth word. When we said, "We, the people of Canada," one hullabaloo broke out in Quebec.

There was one great scandal, because we started the preamble with the words, "We, the people of Canada." The outrage of not only Premier Lévesque but of Quebec intelligentsia and the Quebec media was enormous. Somehow we could not even talk about "the people" of Canada. Of course, it was forbidden to talk about one Canadian "nation", but we found that we could not even mention the people of Canada without offending the Premier of Quebec. Now, I ask you: Do you expect that we could have reached an agreement with the government of that province when we were trying to get a constitution for the Canadian people?

Unfortunately, I go back to Senator Murray, at page 2A:2 of his testimony of August 4. He says:

> . . . in September 1980, Prime Minister Trudeau was willing to recognize "the distinctive character of Quebec society with its French-speaking majority" in a preamble to the Constitution, and a "best-efforts" draft to achieve this end was produced.

Prime Minister Mulroney goes a step further, and is even more wrong. He says the same things in his October 21, 1987 speech to the House of Commons, but he leaves out the words "in a preamble." The allegation is made by these two distinguished gentlemen that I had offered to recognize the distinctive character of Quebec's society with its French-speaking majority. Therefore, what was wrong with doing it in an interpretative clause of the Langevin accord?

I will ask historians to go back to the record on this one, because I have a lot of papers here and I will not pretend to sum them up. However, they are available for anyone who would like to follow it up. They are papers which were distributed to the provinces and, therefore, are not secret. They can be found, I am sure, by asking in the House of Commons. I inquired of the officials in Ottawa where Senator Murray had obtained his information. All the evidence they were able to dig up — and I have a letter here from the secretary to the cabinet sending it to me — is a document entitled "Federal-Provincial Conference of First Ministers, being a report of the continuing committee of ministers on the Constitution, to first ministers."

In the preamble, which is not a very good one, there are square brackets between two phrases, which are obviously phrases where no agreement had been reached and they were referred to the First Ministers for a decision. One phrase is "recognizing the distinct French-speaking society centred in, though not confined to, Quebec." The other phrase is "recognizing the distinctive character of Quebec society with its French-speaking majority." In the first case, "recognizing the distinct French-speaking society centred in, though not confined to, Quebec," if it is a sociological fact, if it is a historical reality put in a preamble, I might not have objected. I probably would not have if it had bought a Charter of Rights in the Constitution. But I am nowhere on record saying that I accepted that. It is in brackets, so it is something to be decided by the First Ministers.

The other phrase, "recognizing the distinctive character of Quebec with its French-speaking majority," that is the one phrase that I never would have put in a preamble, let alone an interpretative clause. Of course, that is the one that comes up in the Meech Lake Accord.

For greater surety, I got a copy of *The Summary Record of Proceedings* of the First Ministers' Conference between September 8 and September 13, 1980. There is an agenda item entitled "The Preamble of Principles." There are three pages dealing with it. It is mainly a quarrel about the people of Canada and whether or not the provinces are freely united.

Mr. Lévesque does go on to say that he objects to the preamble, because it did not, in his view, "accurately reflect the duality which lay at the base of Confederation." Consequently, the Quebec government suggested the following wording:

Recognizing the distinct character of the people of Quebec which, with its French-speaking majority, constitutes one of the foundations of Canadian duality.

Now, perhaps, we know where the idea of duality came from for the 1987 accord.

As far as the chairman is concerned — that is me — I raised two items of concern, which I have just quoted to you. In the conclusion I do not draw any consensus, because there is no agreement amongst anyone. To draw out of that the authority to say that Trudeau was willing to recognize the distinctive character of Quebec society, with its distinctive French-speaking majority, is really going a bit far.

I would like to deal with the difference between the five Quebec demands as met in the 1987 accord and the way they were met before in various attempts, always trying to trade something in exchange for something else, something the present federal government did not do, which I will get into if I have time. Over a period of ten years we were trying to negotiate. We would offer one thing. If it would not work, we would try something else. We would take the first one back and put something else on the table, always trying to trade to get a patriation of the Canadian Constitution.

To take all those things as a whole and say, "You were prepared to give them all when they were completely different. So why are you objecting to the 1987 accord now?" is really an operation in duplicity or ignorance. There is a great difference, because what do we have with the Meech Lake Accord?

Duality vs. Bilingualism

In paragraph 2(1)(a) there is linguistic duality. In subsection 2(2) there is the role of Parliament and legislatures to preserve the duality. Duality divides groups. We did not use the expression "French-speaking Canadians" and "English-speaking Canadians" in any of our constitutions. We used the concept of bilingualism. Bilingualism unites people; dualism divides them. Bilingualism means you can speak to the other; duality means you can live in one language and the rest of Canada will live in another language, and we will all be good friends, which is what Mr. Lévesque always wanted. You speak English, we will speak French, and we will be friends. That is an option. It was a respectable one, one that I fought, but we knew what it meant.

I think we should know what it means also in the Meech Lake Accord. That is subsection 2(2) on linguistic duality and the role of Parliament and the legislatures to preserve that duality. No wonder the French-speaking minorities in the rest of Canada and the English-speaking minorities in Quebec do not like it, and some of them feel "humiliated."[47]

Paragraph 2(1)(b) says that Quebec constitutes within Canada a distinct society. Subsection 2(3) mentions the role of the legislature and government to preserve and *promote* that distinct society, including, as I will read to you later, the right to self-determination, which is part of the deal, according to Mr. Bourassa. I am anticipating myself.

What does Meech Lake mean? First, it is amusing to notice that subsection 2(4) says that this section does not derogate from powers, rights or privileges of Parliament or legislatures.[48] Of course, the sections where the federal government is giving up its authority over the Senate, over the courts, and over the spending power do derogate from federal powers. But this particular subsection does not. The provincial politicians are protecting their turf. It happens again in paragraph

101E(2), where there is no derogation from powers of Parliament over the Supreme Court. After all that Parliament has given away in paragraphs 101A to E, it says, in paragraph 101E(2), "except for what we have just given away on the Supreme Court, nothing will derogate from our powers."

Paragraph 106A(2) says that nothing extends the powers of Parliament or the legislatures on the spending power. After it had just *reduced* the power of Parliament, it says, "nothing extends the powers of Parliament or the legislatures." Politicians are very generous with themselves when they are in power, but what is the effect of these clauses on the Canadian people? Well, we do not know. Because "distinct society" was not put in the preamble, but it was put in an operative clause, in an interpretative clause, we do know that it is a clear instruction to the court as to how they should interpret every other part of the Constitution.

New Powers to Quebec

Since the business of the court is to interpret laws, we must ask ourselves: How will the courts interpret this particular section? Opinions are divided. You have had experts, as have the House of Commons, saying, "Well, it is an interpretative clause; it does not mean anything," or, "It is an interpretative clause; it can mean a lot." We have different opinions even amongst people around here. I will read Senator Murray again on 2:A2 of the same date. He states:

> Let us be clear on two points. Nothing in the proposed amendment changes the distribution of powers between the federal and provincial governments.

Nothing changes distribution of powers.

> Nor does anything in the proposed amendment override the Canadian Charter of Rights and Freedoms, including women's equality rights.

If I can read English, it means that the proposed amendment of "distinct society" and French and English duality does not change anything. It is there to make Quebec feel good, I suppose, but nothing changes. The joint committee is a little less categorical.

First, you have read what they say on page 51. I am reading from the 1987 Constitutional Accord report of the Special Joint Committee of the Senate and the House of Commons at the top of page 51. It states:

> . . . in law the "distinct society" clause is unlikely to erode in any significant way the existing entrenched constitutional rights —

It shows a little less certainty than Senator Murray, but then you get to the "Distribution of powers", on page 45, paragraph 64, and there is even more uncertainty. Quite frankly, I do not like it, because, although it goes in my direction, the joint committee is not taking the responsibility for saying something. It states:

> It might therefore appear difficult to see how the "linguistic duality, distinct society" clauses could affect the division of powers without derogating from the powers, rights or privileges of one level of government in favour of the other.

They are protected by the famous section 2(4). They go on to say:

> Nevertheless, the Joint Committee was advised —

"We are not taking responsibility for this and we are not doing anything about it, but we were advised that:"

> The definition of the scope of the legislative power is an ongoing process of allocating subject matters to heads

of jurisdiction. Take, for example, the regulation of markets for financial securities. Would such a law be classified as an aspect of the federal ''trade and commerce'' power, as some say, or of ''property and civil rights'' within exclusive provincial jurisdiction, as others contend? And what about a new law purporting to regulate the content of radio or television broadcasting?

Yet, there is nothing in the Constitution about broadcasting.[49] The Fathers of Confederation had not read Jules Verne, and there is nothing in there about aviation as well as a lot of other things that they have not thought about. What about a new law on those matters? It goes on to state:

> As new laws are made and challenged before the courts this process of classification of laws into federal or provincial jurisdiction continues. The court docket is limited only by the imagination and productivity of Canada's legislators and lawyers. The ongoing process of the constitutional ''classification'' of laws by the courts is one of the important areas where the interpretative provisions of the ''linguistic duality'' and ''distinct society'' clauses will come into play.

This is not a preamble. These are ''interpretative provisions of linguistic duality'' and ''distinct society'' which will come into play. Indeed, if this were not so, then the ''linguistic duality'' and ''distinct society'' interpretative provisions would be meaningless — a result that can hardly have been intended by its framers, except, of course, Senator Murray!

Really, the Joint Committee was advised of this and came to no conclusion, but they were honest enough to say it. Other people were even more honest. Read Premier Bourassa. This is from June 18, and is on page 8708, *Proceedings of the National Assembly*.[50]

This is what Mr. Bourassa had to say, and I quote:

— the entire Constitution, including the Charter, will be interpreted and applied in the light of this section on the distinct society. The exercise of legislative authority —

So, not only the Charter but also legislative powers.

The exercise of legislative authority is included, and we will thus be able to consolidate existing positions and make new gains.

Page 9031 also elaborates on that.

Mr. Bourassa's Minister for Federal-Provincial Relations, Senator Murray's counterpart, was quite clear, also on June 19, at page 8784. He states:

— the distinct society gives us a tool with which to interpret and give real significance to this sharing of legislative authority, because there are grey areas and ambiguities.

In other words, sections 91 and 92 do not say it all. The courts will use the "distinct society" clause to say, "Well, because Quebec is a 'distinct society' it can extend its rights in this or that direction." Mr. Rémillard[51] goes on and gives examples where Quebec's powers can be extended into broadcasting, banking — the very example of the joint committee report about the economic matters — and international relations. On that matter he says:

The possibility of expressing our views very clearly on the international scene in terms of our specific identity.

I suppose we can say that there is disagreement. At best, this clause is a prescription for discord, but, at worst, it says

Gil Rémillard, minister of intergovernmental affairs, tells the Quebec National Assembly in June 1988 that the province would ensure that the federal bilingualism bill will not interfere with Quebec's powers over languages.   *(Canadian Press)*

that Quebec will evolve under a different constitutional rule than the rest of Canada, because only Quebec is a "distinct society." Therefore, when it comes to a matter of interpreting the Constitution for Quebec, there is more than the possibility, there is a probability that the Constitution will be interpreted differently for Quebec than for the rest of Canada. I will come back to that in a moment when I talk about the consequences of this, but I want to draw a conclusion now. Quebec's five demands were all met in ways which weakened the fabric of Canada by denying the existence of a national will over and above the will of the provinces. The 1987 accord brings us back to the "compact" theory of the 1927 conference, that Canada exists as a country not by the will of its people but by the leave of ten provincial governments. To those who say that what we proposed in the 1970s had this consequence, I say that they did not go back to read what we said, or when they went back they made things up.

The Negotiations

I come now to the negotiations. I would like to leave time for questions also.

It is important to point out that not one of the five demands was correcting some injustice that had been caused to Quebec in 1982. I am not blaming Quebec — I have always said that is it the job of provincial premiers to try to get more powers. It is the nature of politicians to think that they can do things better than politicians at some other level. However, Quebec was making five demands — not, once again, because it had suffered injustices in the 1981 deal, but because it wanted completely new powers. The proof that Quebec was not badly treated in 1981 is that it was not attempting to correct the things that happened in 1981; the whole operation was one of leverage; of trying to tell Canada that it could have its Constitution providing it gave the Province of Quebec more power. That was the sole grievance after the negotiations of 1981 and the Constitution Act, 1982. Quebec had not succeeded in using its leverage to acquire more power. That is where Mr. Lévesque went wrong. He had ganged up with the other seven and had tried to bargain; he was ditched by his partners, and therefore he was not able to bargain for all that he wanted.

However, what he had bargained for within the "gang of eight" was, as I said earlier, largely given to him. So, I repeat, it was not that Quebec was short-changed; it was that Quebec did not get as much power as it was hoped it could have had if it had found in Ottawa a Prime Minister who believed in the "compact" theory.

As for Mr. Bourassa, he was perfectly justified in trying to get more power, because Mr. Mulroney had declared during the 1984 election, and I quote:

> We will have to make commitments to convince the Quebec government to give its consent to the new Canadian Constitution.

It was really up to Mr. Bourassa to trade in that consent for the most power he could get for his province. I always thought he would get some. After all the things we offered in the 1970s, he should be able to get some. I did not think he had much hope for the veto, because he, himself, had thrown it away in 1971, and then Mr. Lévesque threw it away in 1981 and had added that all provinces were equal. Therefore, I thought Mr. Bourassa would fight for it, get, perhaps, four out of the five demands, and grudgingly rejoin the constitutional family.

However, I knew one thing: I knew that the Prime Minister of Canada was in a superb negotiating position. He had compaigned on a program of national reconciliation; he had won with the largest majority in history; he could have convened a federal-provincial conference to end constitutional squabbles, and told all of the premiers that they had better cooperate or else the Canadian people would conclude that the past ten years of bickering were not Trudeau's fault after all, since, even with a nice, new Prime Minister, the premiers were proving to be as quarrelsome as ever. Instead of doing that, he made it clear that he was the one who needed peace at all costs.

Then, I think, everyone must have watched in disbelief, because even *before* the constitutional talks got underway, he proceeded to throw away all of the trump cards he had: Premier Lougheed wanted the abolition of the National Energy Program; he got it. Mr. Peckford wanted administration of the offshore resources that we had only offered to share with him; he got it. Mr. Johnson wanted to sit in at international summits; he got it, and then it was inherited by Mr. Bourassa. Mr. Peterson wanted to be involved in the free trade negotiations; he got that, too. Even President Reagan got the dismantling of FIRA and the abolition of the National Energy Program even before they were sitting down to discuss acid rain.

Therefore, in such circumstances, the Prime Minister of Canada and his entire cabinet were absolutely no match for Bourassa and his able Minister of Intergovernmental Relations, Mr. Rémillard. Soon after the 1985 election Mr. Bourassa really judged with whom he was negotiating, and he moved in for the kill. When Meech Lake was all over, Mr. Bourassa was able to say — and I quote from the *Toronto Star* of May 4, 1987, under the byline of Robert McKenzie. This quote is *en anglais*, I am sorry, but it is contained in the *Toronto Star*.

We didn't expect, after 20 years, to reach an agreement. Then suddenly without warning, there it is — an agreement . . .

We could have waited until next year; we could have waited until after the next federal election. We were under no pressure. I was serene, but when I saw that it was falling to us piece by piece, I said to myself "Bien voilà! There it is."

Justice Minister Pierre Trudeau and Prime Minister Lester Pearson in Ottawa during the Federal-Provincial Constitutional Conference, February 1968. To Trudeau's right, his then senior advisor, Marc Lalond (*Public Archives Canada*)

So much for the federal government's argument, picked up by many of the provinces, that there was and still is a great urgency to the whole matter. Bourassa could have waited until after the next election; why shouldn't we? As for Mr. Mulroney's so-called negotiating skills, I think they should be assessed in the light of Mr. Bourassa's further comment, made at the same press conference, to the effect that he had obtained more in the field of immigration and in the appointment of Supreme Court Justices than he had been seeking. At that point in the press conference Mr. Rémillard chimed in and said that Mr. Bourassa, at the meeting table, successfully argued for even tougher wording, which made the "distinct society" clause more powerful than Quebec had originally dared hope. In short, on three of Quebec's five demands — namely, immigration, Supreme Court and the distinct society — Quebec got more than it was asking for. Yet, for good measure, the Prime Minister throws in two items not asked for: the Senate, which we know about, and federal-provincial conferences, of which there were to be two per year, with an agenda which is fixed until the end of time — or, at least, until there is an agreement between Parliament and seven legislatures to change it. However, until the end of time, you will have on the agenda — with no sunset clause — fisheries and the Senate.

It is no small wonder that Premier Pawley could say — and I am quoting now from the Winnipeg *Free Press* under the byline of Francis Russell:

> The Prime Minister did a very good job of mediating. He was fair and sensitive throughout. He did not try to bully or pressure us at all.[52]

No, he did not try to pressure the provinces into accepting more powers; no sir, he would not do that.

Premier Pawley goes on:

Quebec Premier Robert Bourassa with a copy of the Meech Lake
constitutional proposals in the province's National Assembly, April
29, 1987.   *(Canadian Press)*

Mulroney never once defended the national government's powers, but I felt he was not unhappy that Peterson and I (Pawley) were doing it.

That is, defending the national government's powers.

The Prime Minister wanted to find an accommodation. He put pressure both ways. While he never really came out, I felt he was sympathetic to us.

That is, Peterson and Pawley —

After all, we were trying to maintain national power.

Very helpful, Mr. Pawley. When the future of this country is decided at a conference of 11 First Ministers, when no one speaks for Canada except a couple of provincial premiers, encouraged by a little wink from the Prime Minister, that is a pretty sombre day.

So Prime Minister Mulroney gave Quebec much more than it had asked for in its Quebec Round. What did the federal government get in exchange? I will have to leave most of that for my next appearance, because I have a lot to say on that subject.

The federal government certainly did not trade what it was giving to the provinces in exchange for a correction of the flaws with which I was reproached by Senator Murray in his above-quoted article in *Le Devoir*, namely, the opting-out provision and the notwithstanding clause. Certainly, even in the constitutionalized agenda you would think that the federal government would have put in one or two items, such as native rights, to be discussed at the next conference, or, at least, some power of value to the federal government. Or was it to be another agenda, where Mr. Mulroney would give the provinces their choice of grabs?

I now refer you to Senator Murray's testimony, at page 210:

I have heard it said that the federal government gained nothing in these negotiations, and that it gave but did not get.

I reject these contentions totally. Canada is the clear and undisputed winner in the current round of constitutional negotiations.

I think it is good to have Quebec in. It would be better if we had it in on better terms. In the short run, it is good; in the long run — I will talk about that in my conclusions.

What did the federal government gain? I will read on. He says, "The strengthening of our country. The reconciliation of Quebec. Opportunities for economic policy coordination and future constitutional reform." You could always have federal-provincial conferences. That is not a great gain in terms of a bargain. You could always call them, so that was not a gain for the federal government. The reconciliation of Quebec? We will see. In terms of the strengthening of our country, I just want to ask the question: How do you make a country stronger by weakening the only government that can talk for all Canadians? That is the story of the 1987 negotiations.

Mr. Mulroney's government of national reconciliation was able to bring temporary peace to federal-provincial relations by negotiating a sweetheart constitutional deal whereby enormous amounts of power were transferred to the provincial governments, and particularly to the premiers — powers over vital institutions of the federal government and power over the people of Canada through a weakening of the Charter.

Viewed in perspective, the negotiations of the previous twenty years had involved much more than the struggle between two levels of government. It had been a struggle to establish the sovereignty of the people over all levels of government, and, by the proclamation of the Constitution Act, 1982, the battle for the people's rights was won. The war was not over, the Charter was not perfect, and we still have no referendum process into the amending formula, but the legal community was seeing to it that the Charter was having a real meaning, and the media was reporting the rights of the people over the rights of government, and people began to discover that they had a community of values, that the bonds of Canadian nationhood existed, and so on.

But that process of constitutionalizing the people of Canada, which had begun in 1982, was stopped in its tracks by the 1987 accord. Eleven heads of government were to meet in secret, in the dead of night, transfer unconscionable amounts of power from the national government to the provinces; submit the whole of the Constitution including the Charter to an interpretative clause which entrenched the primacy of two collectivities, and, finally, decreed that no amount of participation by the people of Canada could ever lead to a modification of that accord or of the Constitution itself.

In 1982 the Quebec *government* was not in, because that government has stood for the division of Canada, but the people of Quebec were in. I refer you to a nice article by one of your colleagues, Senator Stollery, in *The Globe and Mail*, dated February 11, 1988, where he makes a tally of those who voted against the 1982 agreement. I do the additions, but the figures are his. Seventy-one Quebec members of Parliament voted for the 1982 Constitution; four of them voted against, and in Quebec's National Assembly, on December 1, 1981, there was a vote as to whether they would or would not condemn Ottawa's and the nine provinces' accord, and 38 courageous Liberals voted against the Péquistes. That is for a total of 109 Quebec elected representatives for the 1982 accord, against a total of 74 against it, four in Ottawa and 70 in Quebec City. That is just tossed out for the benefit of some of those professors who teach that, somehow, Quebec was not in in 1982. It was in legally, and everyone knows that it was in legally and constitutionally. Some people have argued that it was not in ''morally'' or ''politically'' — I think those are the words of the former President of the Canadian Bar Association, Mr. Yves Fortier.[53] Personally, I do not accept that distinction. Let us count heads of elected representatives and you will see that the Quebecers voted in favour of the 1982 accord.

Under the 1987 accord, the Quebec government is in, but the Quebec people stand divided from the rest of Canada as a distinct society. In 1982 there had been a victory of people over power; 1987 was a triumph of power over people.

The Supreme Court, at some point, is going to have to decide, does "distinct society" mean something or does it not? By the time they will have decided it will be too late, either the Quebec nationalists will have been had or the Canadian people will have been had, because if it is decided that "distinct society" and "duality" — linguistic duality — do not mean anything, then the government of Quebec will revert to the position it was in after 1982. It will be bound legally by the accord. But do you think it will be in politically and morally? Do you think Quebec is going to accept that it has been fooled by this phoney drafting, and that it will accept a decision by some five, six or seven judges of the Supreme Court — whatever is a majority, named by Ottawa, "centralizers", "Anglos" for the most part — that "distinct society" has no meaning? Do you think that is a prescription for peace?

If the courts decide that "distinct society" has no meaning, won't we be in exactly the position we were in after 1982, where Quebec was bound legally, as it will be by the 1987 accord, but where some people will argue that it is not bound morally and it is not bound politically?

We have Senator Murray again saying that he could not vote for the 1982 accord because, in conscience, he thought it was not right. I hope that some of you feel that, in conscience, this 1987 accord is not right, either. Senator Murray said, "Without Quebec's participation in our constitutional family, Canada's future would remain in doubt." It will remain in doubt now, believe me, if the Supreme Court goes against it in a deal it thought it made, in a deal that Bourassa and Rémillard spelled out in so many words in the legislative assembly of Quebec. They may say, "He said it meant this and now the courts are saying we were fooled, we were had, we were tricked." Yves Fortier said, "Politically and morally the Constitution Act, 1982 does not apply to Quebec. Those who claim it does are guilty of constitutional heresy."[54] This brings the matter back to the type of reasoning we heard from the Supreme Court in 1981 where it was decided it was legal to go to Westminster, but it was not nice.

But it will not be nice if Quebec has been had in this deal. "Distinct society" would not have any force in law, but it would have tremendous force in the politics of separation, because already Mr. Bourassa, in the quotes I was reading to you, was warned by the then opposition leader, Johnson:

You will have to pay for this.[55]

"You will have to pay for this. . ." if you don't get from Ottawa what you were supposed to get. I do not think Mr. Parizeau[56] will be any more gentle than Mr. Johnson.

Two Constitutions, Two Charters, Two Canadas

What if, on the other hand, the courts decide that "duality" and "distinct society" do have meaning? I think Canadians would discover, to their surprise, that the accord has empowered one provincial government to subordinate the rights of every individual Canadian living within its borders to the rights of a chosen community, presumably, the French-speaking majority. I know what that would do to French-speaking Canadians in other provinces, and I think they know. You cannot go around saying that the Anglos will not have a right to put English even on the French signs in Quebec, but, in the rest of Canada, we are asking you

Parti Quebecois leader Jacques Parizeau attacks the federal
government's bilingualism policy, August 1988.   *(Canadian Press)*

English Canadians to be good, and bilingualism is the way of the future. So we will have what? The possibility of building one Canada will be lost forever. Canada henceforth will be governed by two Constitutions, one to be interpreted for the benefit of Canada and one to be interpreted for the preservation and promotion of Quebec's distinct society — two Constitutions, two Charters, promoting two distinct sets of values, and eventually two Canadas — well, one Canada and something else.

And lest the mistake be made of assuming that the Quebec Round gave Quebec everything that it wanted, we already have Mr. Bourassa in the Legislative Assembly on June 23, reported at page 9031, telling the Leader of the Opposition:

> May I remind the Leader of the Opposition there will be a second round?

No. That staunch federalist, Premier Bourassa, had made his position very clear in the Legislative Assembly on June 18, at page 8709. He said:

> . . . the Liberal Party recognizes Quebec's right . . . to freely express [the] desire to maintain or put an end to the federal union with Canada. Basically, it recognizes the right of the people of Quebec to determine their future as they see fit.

He had just got Meech Lake and Langevin — the works. But, "We still have a right to be independent. We have just signed a marriage contract, but clause I says I can divorce at any time."

So our government of national reconciliation will have bungled its way into a no-win situation for Canada. There will be a showdown if this thing goes through. I know what is going to happen; but, as I was saying earlier, there are still some blunt tools left in the BNA Act: disallowance, taxation — all modes of taxation; the declarative clause; expropriation for federal purposes, and so on. I would not like to be here to have to use them, but I can tell you one thing: it will be the end of the "*peaceable* kingdom." And it is in vain that hundreds of thousands of French-speaking Canadians will have settled in the rest of Canada and tried to preserve their identity; it will be in vain that Acadians will have fought for generations against indifference and frequent hostility; and it will be in vain that many generations of Quebec politicians will have fought for the establishment of the French fact in Canada — not in Quebec, in Canada. I refer to Henri Bourassa, the great Bourassa; and *Le Devoir*, in those days fighting for the rights of various French-speaking communities dispersed throughout Canada (e.g., St. Boniface in Manitoba, Rivière de la Paix in Alberta and Maillardville in British Columbia).

That dream will be gone. And even those who thought they could show that "French power" could exist in Ottawa, that it was not such a forbidding place to French Canadians, will find it to have been in vain. It will be in vain also that many thousands, and even hundreds of thousands, of Canadian children will have learned French across the provinces in immersion courses,[57] because they thought that this could be a country working on the basis of two official languages, bilingualism rather than dualism; that they could be united. So, in vain, we would have dreamt the dream of one Canada.

In Conclusion

So what do we do with the conclusion? Well, the 1987 accord is unlike the parson's egg; it is not only bad in part, it is completely bad. I think it should be put out in the dust bin. And of course the Quebec nationalists will be pretty mad, and there will be some wishy-washy federalists who will be pretty mad, too — those who want to eat their cake and have it too. We should simply remind them of two things: First, that provincial governments have been holding up the process of constitutional reform for 80 years, and, in particular, that Premier Lesage of Quebec backed out of a deal in 1964, Premier Bourassa backed out of a deal in 1971, and Mr. Lévesque was left on the corner by his seven partners in 1981. But no one broke down and wept. Once again, these experts from Queen's or Toronto, or elsewhere, say that "Quebec is in a state of anguish since the 1982 accord because it wasn't in." Not so. Life went on in the province. Sure, the Quebec nationalists will be a bit frustrated if the accord does not go through. That's the real world: "You don't always get what you want. You were offered it before, but you didn't take it. Now we are not offering it to you."

But more important, the second point is that Mr. Bourassa himself said that he could have waited until after the next federal election. Well, my conclusion is that we should do precisely that.

What Can the People Do?

In the meantime, what can be done by the people, by the provincial legislatures and by the Senate? Well, the people should demand that every candidate in every federal or provincial election or by-election should state his or her position on the accord. The Meech Lake Accord had not been debated in any Parliament or legislature before being agreed to in April 1987 by the 11 First Ministers. Therefore, the people should ensure that the same mistake is not made again, that it will be debated. And only if a majority of federal MPs want to campaign in favour of the accord, and if they win their seats, then the governments of Canada and the provinces can put Meech Lake into the Constitution by using the amending process that exists.

That is what the people can do. They have the right to vote, and they have the right to know what their members of Parliament or the legislatures stand for from here on in. It has been done in New Brunswick already, and it is being done now in Manitoba — and I admire the courage and the independence of mind of a Premier McKenna or a Sharon Carstairs, who have the courage to stand up — not against Quebec, but to ask what the Meech Lake Accord means; and they want to make sure that they stand up for Canada after they have been told what it means.

What Can MPPs Do?

So in the provincial legislatures, where the accord is not yet passed, members should consider that any amendment to the Constitution of Canada imparts a new orientation to Canada's destiny. So, voting on it should be a matter of conscience and not of partisanship. Members of those legislatures should force the government to ask for a reference to the Supreme Court, as was done by three provinces in 1980-81.

Before voting on constitutional amendments which will bind Canada for all time, the members have a right to know what will be the effect of the ''distinct society'' clause on women, or on the Charter in general, or on the linguistic minorities. They have a right to know. You don't vote when it is obvious that even the experts don't agree; and when negotiators in Quebec say the accord means one thing and senators in the federal government say exactly the opposite. They have the right to know what is the meaning of such phrases as ''programs or initiatives compatible with national objectives.'' They have a right to know if the doctrine of necessity can be invoked if there is a paralysis of the Supreme Court.

So, in provinces where there might be an election of a new premier who had not signed the accord, and in those that have not yet decided, they should make a reference to the Supreme Court. That is in the law; that is in the practice. And I say, once again, that it is a matter of dignity for a member of the legislature not to vote on something the meaning of which he does not know; and if ever there was a case where the meaning of the Constitution was not clear, it is in the case before us now. So before they vote, let us get a reference. One was obtained in the 1980-81 period. It took something in the order of three or four months, and then we knew. On the occasion we still have another two years or more before time runs out.

What Can the Senate Do?

What can the Senate do? Well, it is too late to use tactics, as you did on me in 1978, to threaten obstruction in order to get a reference, which we gave you. I do not think you have the time between now and April 23 to obstruct in any meaningful way. I suggest that the Senate pass amendments that will ensure that the resolution is corrected so that it means, if you believe in it, what Senator Murray says it does mean, that "distinct society" has no effect on the Charter or on the distribution of powers. That is the minimum amendment that you can make, but there are many others that, for a fee, I would be prepared to suggest to you.

Unless you fear that you are offending someone, remember the Langevin accord, paragraph 1 of the operative sector, which states:

> The Prime Minister of Canada will lay or cause to be laid before the Senate and House of Commons, and the first ministers of the provinces will lay or cause to be laid before their legislative assemblies, as soon as possible, a resolution, in the form appended hereto —

So they did that. They did not say the Senate could not amend it. They did not say the members of the House of Commons could not amend it. They tried to amend it. The Liberal Party proposed amendments that were not carried, but nothing in the accord says that the Senate cannot amend it.

I would suggest that if you want to know what you are voting on, you should make it clear and say what you think "distinct society" means, and maybe even within this chamber

Liberal leader John Turner, Prime Minister Brian Mulroney and NDP leader Ed Broadbent defend the Meech Lake Accord in the House of Commons on June 14, 1988.   *(Canadian Press)*

you will find that some Quebecers do not agree with some Ontarians on what it means, I do not know, but the stock and trade of legislatures, from time immemorial, has been to vote on something the meaning of which they assume they know and then when they realize they do not know they clarify it with an amendment.

Therefore, I conclude that the Senate can and must send an amended resolution back and ask the House of Commons to vote on that.

There is nothing in the Constitution of 1982 that says the Senate has to believe exactly the same thing as the members of the House of Commons. So, if you want clarification, you should amend it and send it back, and the members of the House of Commons can discuss whether the clarification has made it worse; but, at least, the people will have been enlightened as to the real meaning of Meech Lake and the real direction in which the country is going.

I think we should take our chances. Let the people decide once they know what it means. If the members of the House of Commons and senators and legislators of the provinces want to vote against the accord because they do not want it, then the accord should be discarded. The Quebec government might be a bit disappointed, but, then, it set the rules. In 1981 Premier Lévesque held that all provinces were equal. That is what they would be: They would get no Meech Lake, but everybody would be equal.

On the other hand, if the people of Canada want this accord, and that is not beyond the realm of possibility, then let that be part of the Constitution. I, for one, will be convinced that the Canada we know and love will be gone forever. But, then, Thucydides wrote that Themistocles' greatness lay in the fact that he realized Athens was not immortal. I think we have to realize that Canada is not immortal; but, if it is going to go, let it go with a bang rather than a whimper.

Chapter Five

Conclusion

By Donald Johnston

In the foregoing, Pierre Trudeau has described two sharply contrasting views of Canada. The Canada we know evolved from the concept of a strong but not overbearing federal authority. It was born of Sir John A. Macdonald's belief that the loose confederation to the south was unacceptable. He saw the United States as an association of sovereign states with delegated authority to a federal government. The folly of such an arrangement was clear, for the country had just struggled through the bloody Civil War of 1860-65. While he personally preferred a simple legislative union as opposed to a federation, those who sought to respect the diversity of the various provinces opted for the federal model. Macdonald reluctantly agreed, provided there would be a strong federal government at the helm.

So it was that through the efforts of Sir George-Étienne Cartier and others, Quebec succeeded in protecting its language, its culture, its religion, its education and its law within the framework of the federation. Those who argue today that these elements make Quebec a distinct society should realize that the sociological distinctiveness of Quebec was recognized in 1867 and has been protected ever since. Whatever advantages accrue to Quebec under Meech Lake must be in addition — as yet undefined.

The strong federal authority envisaged by our Fathers of Confederation has been eroded by judicial interpretation. But the whole has always remained greater than the sum of its parts. For all the squabbling and turf protection that characterizes a federal system, Canada has been a remarkable success. How often must we remind ourselves of our position among the leading industrial nations of the world? It is our federalism which has brought benefits to all Canadians irrespective of where they live. Equalization payments transferring wealth from the have- to the have-not provinces, unemployment insurance and health insurance are but some of the equitable distribution programs federalism has provided. Add to that our bilingual and multicultural heritage which Canadians are gradually coming to see as a national treasure rather than an obstacle to unity and progress. This is the Canada with a "national will" that Pierre Trudeau describes.

The other Canada, that of Meech Lake, is one we have never known. As Trudeau points out, it is a legitimate option, but one he rejects. It can be likened more to confederation of sovereign states where the country is merely the sum of its constituent elements. The federal government becomes an administrative unit for the coordination and implementation of policies and jurisdictions delegated to it by the provinces. Under this framework the federal government may be likened to a condominium manager with responsibility delegated by the owners to take care of the common property, cut the grass, remove the snow and clean the lobby and hallways. For those who decry our lack of breast-beating patriotism so evident in the United States, it will never be found through the Meech Lake approach.

Indeed, Trudeau's submissions demonstrate:

- If you believe in *One Canada* you must reject Meech Lake.
- If you believe that this country should hold a national vision that is greater than the sum of provincial visions, that is,

a Canada greater than the sum of its provincial parts, you must reject Meech Lake.

- If you believe that the individual minority rights of Canadians, be they linguistic rights or sexual equality rights, should be protected against the collective rights of a distinct society, you must reject Meech Lake.

- If you believe that Canada requires national programs meeting national standards or criteria in such areas as research, education, training, income maintenance, childcare and health, you must reject Meech Lake.

- If you believe the Constitution should be a flexible instrument responding to changing economic and social conditions as our country evolves with an amending formula to allow that to happen, you must reject Meech Lake.

- If you believe that the eleven First Ministers should not have the power to determine the future of Canada in private session behind closed doors and then impose this consensus on Parliament, provincial legislatures and the country, you must reject Meech Lake.

- If you believe that the judges of the Supreme Court should not be appointed only from candidates submitted by provincial governments, you must reject Meech Lake.

- If you believe the Senate should be reformed to reflect the original intentions of the Fathers of Confederation, namely, to protect the regions against the possibility of an overbearing central authority, you must reject Meech Lake.

- If you believe that in a federation like ours the provinces should exercise the same powers and that no province should have a special legal status which entitles it to exercise important powers not available to other provinces, you must reject Meech Lake.

- If you see our country as one with two official languages and bilingual institutions in every province with protection for linguistic minorities, you must reject Meech Lake.

Meech Lake is not yet a reality but its spirit is alive and prospering. Saskatchewan saw fit to eliminate the legal rights of its linguistic minority which predated its status as a province. Why not? Its only obligation under Meech Lake is to "preserve the existence of French-speaking Canadians," certainly not to preserve their *rights*.

A more celebrated case is, without doubt, Bill 178 adopted by the Bourassa government to counter the Supreme Court decision on bilingual signage. Bourassa advised the country that had Meech Lake been in effect, he would not have resorted to the "notwithstanding clause" because he could have accomplished the same objectives through the additional powers granted to Quebec by Meech Lake. This extraordinary move to suppress freedom of expression within the province seems to have been instrumental in turning national public opinion against the Accord. The spirit of Meech Lake was again revealed in all its ugliness, and Canadians didn't like it.

Canada does not belong to eleven First Ministers who come and go as the public trust is offered or withdrawn. They must not be allowed to abuse the temporary role of trustee by surreptitiously putting constitutional evolution, the face and shape of Canada and its public institutions, beyond the will of the people.

How can this juggernaut be arrested? Only through informing the Canadian public. Public opinion plays a greater role in the political process than ever before. Pierre Elliott Trudeau's statements will contribute to that process. If the Meech Lake Accord is ratified in 1990, it will be too late to reclaim the dream of One Canada. It is up to Canadians to speak out, to influence political leadership before it is too late.

Postscript

A Dialogue Between Pierre Trudeau, Marcel Adam, and Claude Morin

Let Meech Lake Be English Canada's Problem

Marcel Adam in La Presse, *Montreal, Saturday, March 4, 1989:*

Premier Bourassa has been accused of seeming too persistent about the Meech Lake Accord. But we've noticed lately that he appears less anxious about the uncertain future of the agreement — this man who once displayed a degree of independence by pointing out that Canada, in fact, has more to lose than Quebec if it doesn't become law.

When Prime Minister Mulroney announced a few weeks ago that the provincial premiers' meeting of last Monday would be held in Ottawa, Mr. Bourassa greeted the news without emotion, as if it was all the same to him whether there was a meeting or not.

I admired this detached attitude and would have liked to see him adopt it long before now. I even surprised myself by wishing privately that something would crop up to make

him miss the meeting, leaving his English-Canadian coun-
terparts to sort out their own problems.

In fact, Quebec hasn't sufficiently emphasized to them
that this Accord is first and foremost Ottawa's and English
Canada's problem. Since many seem to have forgotten, it's
worth recalling that the Meech Lake Constitutional Accord
is a gesture of reparation to Quebec, subsequent to the bad
bargain for which it footed the bill at the time of the 1981
negotiations for repatriation of the Constitution.

The day after the (1980) referendum, making a pretext
of the fact that he and several English-Canadian premiers
had made the commitment during the referendum campaign that a "no" would be interpreted as a "yes" to
constitutional reform, Trudeau (sic) undertook a reform
that would end by being imposed on Quebec against the
wishes of its government, and to the detriment of her
legislative powers.

The word *fraud* is not too strong a description for a
political power play that was without precedent here — and
perhaps unprecedented in any other federal democracy —
intended to impose a reform on Quebec that produced a
result contrary to that anticipated from the contract entered
into to keep her in the federation.

Because Quebec was the victim here, because those who
isolated Quebec were themselves trapped by being deprived
of her essential contribution on certain pressing constitutional reforms, the ball is now in the court of Ottawa and
the other nine provinces. It's up to them to make reparation.
Nor should Quebec act as if this isolation has begun to weigh
more heavily on her than on those who betrayed her.

All of which leads to this. Premier Bourassa was wise to
participate in Monday's meeting. How appropriate that the
MacKenna-Filmon duo should meet at the same table with
the nine signatories to the Accord and that Robert Bourassa
should address their objections to the concessions made to
Quebec.

But I'm not sure that Mr. Bourassa should participate

again in an exercise that must be repeated three more times between now and the fall.

Monday's meeting left everyone where they already stood. The signatories did not wish to reopen the Accord to negotiation for fear of its demise. The two who had not signed were not won over and gave no sign of budging.

They actually gave the impression that they thought time was on their side. "I'm waiting for them to show some flexibility" asserted Gary Filmon. He meant Robert Bourassa, who is the cornerstone of this Accord.

My feeling is that Bourassa's participation in (more of) these meetings can only sustain the dissenters' hopes of finally winning their case, thereby backing them into a corner from which they'd be unable to move without losing face, should they find at the end of the proceedings that they'd misjudged the Quebec premier's determination.

A good way of conveying an unequivocal message to one's colleagues can be to let them go whistle.

Robert Bourassa should tell his co-signatories that the outcome of Meech Lake is their problem from now on. It would then be up to them to convince the skeptics that the Accord is an act of reparation to Quebec and that it's an illusion to expect their premier to accept a weak compromise — something that would amount to political suicide (for him).

(Yet) I seem to be going to a lot of trouble for an accord about which I've expressed several reservations. My reticence comes not from the fear that it will be bad for Quebec but that it will be (bad) for Canada in the long run. But, like most other people so far, I'm sure of nothing in this respect. That's what makes this Accord so unusual: no one, including those who created it, interprets it in the same way.

If, as the government and the federalist intelligentsia of Quebec believe, the Meech Lake Accord is the best way of putting right the mess of 1981, Mr. Bourassa should not act as if he had forgotten the historical circumstances that made it necessary.

And it is no less important for Quebec to make Ottawa and the other provinces realize that Canada has more to lose then Quebec by leaving the province isolated, as she has been for eight years now.

Because the Trudeau reform was contemptuous in style and fraudulent in content, Quebec has every right to expect reparation. The Quebec government must always take steps to ensure that its partners never forget this.

The 1982 Constitution Act Was Not a Bad Bargain for Quebec

Pierre Elliott Trudeau in La Presse, *Montreal, Friday, March 10, 1989.*

Sir:

Your reporter, Marcel Adam, used a very offensive word in *La Presse* on March 4 when referring as follows to the 1982 Constitution Act:

> The word *fraud* is not too strong a description for a political power play that was without precedent here — and perhaps unprecedented in any other federal democracy — intended to impose a reform on Quebec that produced a result contrary to that anticipated from the contract entered into to keep her in the federation.

So the accusation is that "Trudeau undertook on the eve of the referendum campaign" a constitutional reform "contrary to (that) anticipated from the contract entered into." And later: "The Trudeau reform was contemptuous in style and fraudulent in content." And then: "a fraudulent bargain for which (Quebec) footed the bill."

What are the facts?

During my 19 years in political life and the 16 years that preceded them, when I was contributing to *Cité Libre* and teaching constitutional law, I always opposed the idea of a "special status" for Quebec.

To be sure, during the referendum campaign, I told Quebecers that in the event of a "no" victory, I would undertake to bring to a successful conclusion the constitutional process initiated in 1967, at the time of the provincial premiers' conference convened by Premier John Robarts at the suggestion of Premier Daniel Johnson.

Now, in all that time, my thinking had not changed. I had always maintained that any reform must begin with the repatriation of the Constitution, to which would be added an amendment formula giving Quebec a right of veto, and a Charter of Rights guaranteeing, among other items, the equal status of the French and English languages. But above all, no special status for Quebec.

Where was the fraud? Where was the bad bargain? The Constitution Act of 1982 did indeed give Canada her own Constitution for the first time and, equally, enshrined a Charter of Rights where articles 16 to 20 affirmed the equality of the French and English languages. It is true that Quebec's right of veto was there only in part (articles 38 (2) and 41), but this was because Premier René Lévesque preferred the amendment formula proposed by Alberta, rather than the absolute veto I had proposed to Mr. Bourassa at the time of the Victoria Conference in 1971 (he turned it down) and again to Mr. Lévesque between 1976 and 1981.

Of course, these were not the reforms advocated by the separatists and those nationalists who wanted a special status for Quebec. But what form of logic would entitle them to believe that an unsuccessful "yes" vote would give rise to the kind of reforms sought by the "yes" side — and against which a majority of the "no" side had always fought?

Premier Lévesque, for his part, clearly understood the

nature of our reforms. Four days before the referendum, in an interview published May 16, 1980 in *Le Devoir*, he said that judging from "Trudeau's recent comments . . . the new formula (would be) as centralizing as ever" (quoted in a Senate speech by Mr. Gigantes on December 20, 1988. The Senator also cited an interview with Jean Chrétien several days before the referendum where this federal minister, then holding the constitutional portfolio, stated that Trudeau's "reformed federalism" presupposed a federal government strong enough to redistribute Canada's wealth, and one that would not grant special status to any single province.)

Once again, Mr. Adam, where was the fraud? When and where did I propose a bad bargain or make false representations to the Quebec electorate — either before, during, or after the referendum?

As for the "power play" that imposed a "contemptuous reform," how do you see it?

From 1927 to 1979, in the course of a long sequence of federal-provincial conferences, every Canadian prime minister tried to replace the British Act of Parliament that served as our Constitution with a truly Canadian Constitution. Each attempt failed because one or more provinces opposed it.

In 1980, the majority of Quebecers rejected the independence option by answering "no" to a subtly worded question (one that some might describe as contemptuous and fraudulent). At that point, the Canadian government judged that, having escaped disintegration, Canada should make a supreme effort to attain formal sovereignty by severing all constitutional ties with Great Britain, and instituting a Charter of Human Rights applicable to all Canadians.

Lengthy negotiations followed . . . But still nothing happened, and in the spring of 1981, the participants were drawn up in two camps: on one side, the P.Q. government plus seven other provinces; on the other side, the federal government plus Ontario and New Brunswick.

After 54 years of failed attempts at repatriation, the federal government decided to cut the Gordian knot: 114 years after Confederation, Canada would declare her independence without the unanimous consent of the provinces.

Power play or legitimate political decision? We would find out: three provinces (including Quebec) asked the Supreme Court that question, obtaining a judgment in September 1981 that stated the action would be legal, but outside constitutional "conventions."

Everyone went back to the negotiating table. The group of eight provinces (Quebec included) made several counter-proposals that were accepted in hopes of achieving unanimity: the "notwithstanding" clause would lessen the scope of the Charter; the Alberta amendment formula would replace that of Victoria; the provinces would acquire some new jurisdictions relating to indirect taxation and international trade. Despite all this, there was still an impasse.

At the beginning of November, the federal side made a proposal that temporarily brought the Quebec government onside, though it did not suit the seven provinces with which Quebec had allied itself. Feeling betrayed, these seven announced that they would seek a compromise solution independently of Quebec. They found their solution but when they presented it to the Quebec government, it was rejected.

For the second time, Canada decided to declare her independence without the provinces' unanimous consent . . .

Power play or legitimate political decision? Once again, we would find out: when Quebec asked the Supreme Court this question, she was told that the action was both legal and constitutionally "conventional" since no one province had the right to veto on its own. The same judgment decreed that Quebec was most certainly bound by the

Canadian Constitution of 1982. (Consequently, there is no need for the Meech Lake Accord's "bringing Quebec into the Constitution"; those who claim the opposite — from Mr. Adam to Mr. Mulroney by way of Mr. Bourassa — are talking nonsense.)

Political checkmate, perhaps. Miscalculation, misalliance, no doubt. But "a fraudulent solution," Mr. Adam? A "power play . . . unprecedented in any other federal democracy"? What federations are these, where the government of only one component could indefinitely keep in check the will of the majority for independence?

What conclusions should we draw from all this?

"In this matter," concludes Mr. Adam, "Quebec is the victim (of) those who isolated her . . ." and he sees "the Meech Lake Accord (as) a gesture of reparation to Quebec." Someone else is always to blame! Weren't those who isolated Quebec in reality the P.Q. government who wanted independence for their province but would deny it to Canada?

Never mind! Mr. Adam demands reparation: nothing less than acceptance of the Meech Lake Accord by all Canadians. An accord that nevertheless evokes in him "the fear that it will be bad . . . for Canada in the long run." An accord in which he deplores the "odd situation" whereby "no one, including those who created it, interprets it in the same way." An accord on which, finally, he seems to share Mr. Bourassa's opinion, to the effect that "Canada has more to lose than Quebec, should it fail to become law."

At last, Mr. Adam, I recognize the honest man inside the outraged nationalist's tatters. Now, please, surprise me! Make one more gesture. Since the Meech Lake Accord is bad for Canada, since Quebec doesn't need it all that much, let's agree that Canada will be better off if the Meech monster goes back and drowns itself at the bottom of the lake from which its ugly head should never have emerged.

The Real Question Is: What Was Quebecers' Understanding of Mr. Trudeau?

Marcel Adam in La Presse, *Montreal, Saturday, March 11, 1989:*

Yesterday Pierre Elliott Trudeau explained at length in these pages how his commitment, during the referendum campaign, to reform the Canadian Constitution should be interpreted.

The important point is not what Mr. Trudeau really had in mind when he gave that commitment but how the people of Quebec interpreted it.

The commitment — indeed the only one — that we all remember was made in good faith at the last of his three public appearances on behalf of the "no" side, at Paul Sauvé Arena on May 14, 1980. Here is what he said:

> I'm solemnly appealing to you Canadians in all the other provinces when I tell you we're putting our heads on the line here by telling Quebecers to vote "no." But we want you to understand that you must not interpret a "no" vote to mean that everything's fine and should remain just as it's always been. We want changes.

I was at that meeting and I couldn't believe my ears. I told myself that Mr. Trudeau must have been really afraid that the "yes" side would win, to have decided to make concessions in an area where he'd always been so uncompromising. The (then) head of the (Quebec) Liberal party and of the "no" side, Claude Ryan, must have had the same thought when he congratulated the man with whom he'd always differed so much on constitutional matters.

That declaration was like a thunderbolt in Quebec. It was the high point of the campaign.

How many Quebecers equated this vague commitment with the idea of more flexibility in terms of Quebec's demands?

After the adoption of the 1982 Constitution Act, Prime Minister Trudeau was accused on all sides in Quebec of having betrayed his commitment to us. The first time Mr. Trudeau ever troubled to respond to this accusation was last year in the Senate at the time of its Meech Lake investigation. He repeated the essence of that response in this paper yesterday.

He could never have considered reforming the Constitution, he said, in such a way as to incorporate changes that he had opposed during 35 years of public life. Above all, he could not accept the idea of a special status for Quebec.

Since his thinking had never changed, Quebecers should have anticipated in any promised reform only those things he had always advocated: repatriation of the Constitution with an amending formula (and right of veto for Quebec), with a Charter of Rights guaranteeing the equality of the French and English languages.

Certainly, initiates in constitutional matters were not taken in by this vague, ambiguous commitment. For myself, I even defended Mr. Trudeau a few months later. You would have to be naive or simply lack understanding of this man, I wrote, to think that he had changed position on constitutional matters. But my analysis did not go far enough.

The question that must be asked is how significant such a commitment was to the majority of Quebecers — people who pay scant attention to constitutional debate.

The referendum was the outcome of a dispute that

originated 20 years earlier in Quebec. All of our federalist premiers, from Lesage to Bourassa, by way of Johnson and Bertrand, had called for fundamental modifications to the Constitution that would permit a new division of powers: that is (to say), one that would give Quebec additional legislative powers for the purpose of better preserving her distinct character.

To Quebecers, then, could the promise of constitutional reform mean anything other than what it meant to their politicians, their leading nationalists, and most of their federalist commentators? The question is even more timely in light of the constitutional proposals of the (Quebec) Liberal party's *Beige Book*, developed under Claude Ryan, (which) had been available for several months (before the referendum) and which opposed Mr. Trudeau's plans (but which he was very careful not to dispute prior to the referendum).

It is useful to underline two points again. On one hand, the prereferendum polls indicated that a large proportion of Quebecers who had decided or were inclined to vote "yes" actually wanted reformed federalism. On the other hand, the "no" side wasn't sure of winning — even several days before the vote, as Jean Chrétien confirms in his memoirs.

Mr. Trudeau was no doubt aware of these things as he prepared to give the speech that could make the difference between victory and defeat. Is it conceivable that, being the fine politician he was, he decided that in the circumstances, an ambiguous commitment to reformed federalism might be interpreted in such a way as to turn a vast number of Quebecers away from the temptation of voting "yes"?

I'm speculating here, and I know that's rather despicable. But by choosing to be vague, Mr. Trudeau has left it to the rest of us to interpret his commitment for good or ill. Which entitles us to posit that he took the calculated risk of winning the referendum on the basis of a misunderstanding . . .

Who Could Imagine Ontario Being Abandoned?

Marcel Adam in La Presse, *Montreal, Tuesday, March 14, 1989:*

Last weekend, Prime Minister Brian Mulroney responded to Pierre Elliott Trudeau's letter about the 1982 Constitution Act, published in these pages last Friday.

Having stated that Canada could not survive without Quebec, Mr. Mulroney added: "Do you suppose for a moment that Mr. Trudeau and his colleagues would have proceeded to repatriate the Constitution in 1981-82 without the consent of Queen's Park (the Ontario legislature)? For me, Canada is not a country without Ontario. So why repatriate the Constitution without Quebec's consent? Quebec is just as important!"

Can you imagine Mr. Trudeau imposing on Ontario a constitutional reform she didn't want? It's the same as imagining an anglophone prime minister imposing the 1982 Constitution Act on Quebec. In either case, it would have been not only political suicide but also extremely risky for the future of the federation.

You'll recall that he did not want to make Ontario subject to Article 133, already in effect in Quebec, allowing the use of both English and French in the legislature as well as the courts. Why? For fear of losing Ontario's support and seeing his venture fail.

(I'm not saying that he should have imposed it — something that many in Quebec clamoured for at the time — because such a demand only weakens a cause in terms of fair play: imposing on others what we find unacceptable ourselves.)

Mr. Trudeau's argument is well known: it was pointless to hope that a separatist government could be made to accept a federal reform.

It is also well known that the P.Q. government — once its electorate had rejected the (independence) option — promised to participate in good faith in the constitutional proceedings initiated by Mr. Trudeau, in an attempt to reform federalism in the light of the demands of all the previous federal governments.

But the federal government, along with many Quebec federalists, had every reason to believe that the (P.Q.) government, in reality, would be incapable of making an effective contribution to reforming the Canadian federation: to do so would betray the party's *raison d'être*.

So, why did Mr. Trudeau undertake to reform Canadian federalism when he had said time and again, after being blocked by the 1978 constitutional conference, that this could never be achieved with a separatist government (in power in Quebec)?

After the "no" victory, he could have advised Quebec and the rest of Canada that he would be unable to fulfil his commitment to reform federalism until the people of Quebec had determined, at forthcoming elections, which party would be negotiating these reforms on their behalf.

Moreover, weren't the polls predicting a big win for the Quebec Liberal Party? Wouldn't this mean the return to power of a federalist party — one that was interested in maintaining the federation, not tearing it down?

But what was desirable in theory was different in practice, because Pierre Trudeau and Claude Ryan did not agree at all on constitutional matters. The reform proposed in the Quebec Liberal Party's *Beige Book* was the very opposite of Mr. Trudeau's proposals.

You might think that Mr. Trudeau had no wish to see Claude Ryan at the negotiating table, since he had already initiated reform proceedings before the elections. So it was that he chose to deal with René Lévesque who — according to (Mr. Trudeau) could not contribute to federal reform.

Unless Mr. Trudeau hoped to find in the P.Q. premier

an ally dedicated to constitutional reform, why did he want him at the table?

Whatever his intention at the time, I'm willing to state that today, (Mr. Trudeau) would be believed for asserting that Quebec was not isolated by its partners; rather, it was the P.Q. government that isolated itself because of its sovereignty option.

Trudeau's Legacy of Bitterness

Claude Morin in La Presse, *Montreal, Tuesday, March 14, 1989:*

Mr. Claude Morin, former P.Q. minister of intergovernmental affairs and author of a book on the constitutional negotiations that followed the 1980 referendum, here replies to former prime minister Pierre Elliott Trudeau. We recall that the latter, in a letter published last Friday by La Presse, *defended the 1982 Constitution Act. This Act was not a bad bargain for Quebec, Mr. Trudeau reaffirmed.*

And so, former prime minister Trudeau has objected to Marcel Adam's accurate statement that the 1980-82 constitutional reform "produced a result contrary to that anticipated from commitments made on behalf (of Quebec)."

What commitments? On May 14, 1980, in the Paul Sauvé Arena, during the referendum campaign, Mr. Trudeau said (the italics are mine):

If it's a "no," it will be interpreted as a mandate to *change the Constitution and reform federalism* . . . I make the solemn commitment that after a "no" (vote), we will activate the mechanism for *constitutional reform* and we will stop only when it is complete . . . We're putting our heads on the line here by telling

Quebecers to vote "no" . . . We want *changes*. We're risking our seats for these *changes*.

Federalists knew very well that in the context of the times and for the general public, there was only one way to interpret these words: a "no" vote meant a "yes" to federal reform, an old Quebec aspiration that Ottawa had committed to make a reality. In effect, the "no" side hastened to define the commitment in this way, even if the expression "reformed federalism," then current in political parlance, had never been part of — was contrary to — the concept of Canada promoted by Mr. Trudeau. So it was by means of his surprising statement, no doubt part of his strategy, and by playing on words, that he misled a lot of Quebecers. What followed soon confirmed this.

Is he trying to make us forget this episode — so ignoble in retrospect — from his political career? The fact remains that today he affirms that he actually:

> told Quebecers that in the event of a "no" victory, I would undertake to bring to a successful conclusion the constitutional process initiated in 1967, at the time of the provincial premiers' conference convened by Premier John Robarts at the suggestion of Premier Daniel Johnson(!)

This (affirmation) is so contrary to the facts that I'm prepared to dare Mr. Trudeau to prove it. His real words are those from the speech at Paul Sauvé, which I have quoted. There are no others.

Moreover, how can we reconcile such a new interpretation of his May 1980 commitment with this other passage in his article where Mr. Trudeau writes that after the "no" vote,

> . . . the Canadian government judged that, having escaped disintegration, Canada should make a su-

preme effort to attain formal sovereignty by severing all constitutional ties with Great Britain, and instituting a Charter of Human Rights applicable to all Canadians(?)

These two versions of the facts are incompatible.

The first point. If, despite the evidence, the argument of the "process initiated in 1967" that he now refers to should be retained, Mr. Trudeau would have to recall that for Quebec, the 1967 undertaking and constitutional reform in general, *initiated by him*, made sense only if they were going to result in a new agreement on the division of powers and a redefinition of Quebec's role in Canada. That was reformed federalism. It had to do with powers and structures. The repatriation of the Constitution came after. I know something about all this: I was in Toronto in 1967 and I had edited the Johnson government's dissertation.

Now, as Mr. Trudeau also claims, if the post-referendum priority was to repatriate the Constitution, making Great Britain insert a Charter of Rights into it, not only did he fail to breathe a word of it in his promises, not only had Quebec never even thought of it, but this procedure was completely opposite to what Quebec had sought in 1967 and the years that followed.

Mr. Trudeau must have sensed that his explanation would not hold. To defend himself, he turns to an unusual source for support. He mentions that Mr. Lévesque, for one, didn't equate his promises with "reformed federalism." And he adds, as rather cynical testimony, that Mr. Lévesque "clearly understood the nature of our reforms"! Stated another way, according to this, since Mr. Lévesque (had) understood what was up, no one in Quebec should have been fooled by the intervention of May 14. What, then, was the purpose of this intervention?

In theory, three hypotheses are possible. The first is clearly absurd: for Mr. Trudeau to have reiterated his inflexible views. That would have given exquisite scope to the "yes" side! The second is ridiculous: he'd come, with much ado, to say nothing — something we must admit is patently not his style. That leaves only the third: he wanted to sway the vote to the "no" side by persuading people that a "no" would result in a more open attitude on his part.

There is no point in seeking any other explanation. The brilliant orator firmly linked a "no" vote to future changes and expressed this in such a way that the public concluded that these changes would be in line with Quebec's expectations. Of course, what followed had nothing to do with the happy outcome that was promised. So it was that the traps were set in the days that followed the referendum.

Was Mr. Trudeau making fun of us all, in his patrician way, in 1980 — only to apologize now for the fact that Mr. Lévesque and other political "initiates" knew how to "decode" him? Perhaps he judged that in essence, he'd fooled only the "uneducated" with his (stated) commitments — these people who for some years (sadly for them) had been unable to understand him. But a point: Mr. Trudeau's "uneducated," at the time of the referendum, comprised a bigger part of the electorate than the "initiates." And it was more susceptible to influence, as the strategists for the "no" side knew perfectly well. Perhaps he was also hoping that these "uneducated" would fail to notice the contradiction between his May 14 message of hope and the perverse results of the post-referendum constitutional arrangements — results from which we're still suffering the consequences today

What did Mr. Trudeau actually take us for? It's a legitimate question when, later in his text, he makes an insinuation that is both typical and absurd. If Quebec was isolated in 1981, he asserts that it was the fault of the P.Q. government at the time "which wanted independence for Quebec but would deny it to Canada."

Wait a minute! Is the former prime minister saying that Quebec would have advocated that Canada's dependence on Great Britain continue, while seeking her own sovereignty? That Quebec would have tried to prevent Canada from becoming independent, so as to retain British domination? Come on, now!

This paradoxical — not to say dishonest — way of presenting things doesn't hold water. Mr. Trudeau has resorted here to one of his favourite tactics: distorting the facts. Since Quebec rejected *his* approach and *his* methods and since these, *in part*, were aimed at severing all ties with Great Britain, our mighty logician concludes that Quebec *therefore* opposed Canada's independence! As if that was the only objective. In 1980-82, this was most certainly not the case, as Mr. Trudeau is well aware. In reality, he believed he had found the golden mean, by making use of the "no" (vote) to fashion Canada according to his dogmatic, definitive view of things. The country's independence served only as a pretext. This was to be a Canada built "for a thousand years" as he affirmed last year before his friends in the Senate.

It was *this vision*, not Canada's independence, that the Parti Québécois opposed, as any Quebec government — including Robert Bourassa's Liberals, feeble as they are — would have done. Witness: now, federalist governments are trying to put right the post-referendum mess by way of the Meech Lake Accord. Shouldn't Mr. Trudeau be explaining to us why, regardless of its value, these governments have gone to the trouble of creating such an accord (which, by the way, shows in retrospect that the Quebec negotiators of the day were right), if he was so successful in 1980-82? Is he — this political Galileo — the *only* one who's right?

And since he's so fond of rational discussion, why not explain to us at the same time where the independence he apparently dreamed of for Canada became inadmissible with that sought by Quebec?

Mr. Trudeau puts forward something else, for example, that after the "no" victory, no one should have anticipated reforms being made that had been favoured by the "yes" side. That is self-evident — and it was not our objective, either as a government or as a party. Like everyone else, we had every right to hope that after his promises of "reformed federalism," Mr. Trudeau would make a sincere effort to show that he hadn't intentionally made fools of the Quebec electorate.

Regardless, we now know that by his subsequent actions, he has bequeathed to Canada and to Quebec a legacy of bitterness, its destructive influence brought home to us almost every day by events and by the media.

Pierre Trudeau Replies: "That's No Way to Write History"

Pierre Elliot Trudeau in La Presse, *Montreal, Wednesday March 22, 1989.*

Sir:

A few paragraphs, please, to reply to the six columns that *La Presse* of March 14 published by way of response to my article of March 10.

In my article, I maintained that my pre-referendum commitments to reform the Constitution could have meant only one thing: reform in the way that I'd never ceased advocating since 1968. So there was never any "fraud" as claimed by Mr. Adam in his March 4 piece.

Then along came Claude Morin. Mr. Trudeau, he said, in substance, promised *Quebecers* reform. Therefore, they had every right to expect it would proceed in the way *Quebec* wanted.

(Mr. Morin conveniently left out that part of my commitment was directed to *other provinces*, those who were also trying to oppose our efforts at constitutional reform. Lysiane Gagnon in *La Presse* of March 11 quoted my complete text; I thank her for anticipating the misrepresentation that Mr. Morin would write four days later: "His actual words . . . I have quoted. There are no others.")

Now, to Mr. Morin, *Quebec* is the entity that expresses itself politically through the voice of the provincial government. There, precisely, is the fallacy. To me, as to all Quebecers who are not separatists, *Quebec* is also the entity that expresses itself politically through the voice of the federal government. That is to say, the government that I happen to have had the privilege of leading, from 1968 to 1984, except for nine months. To believe Quebecers incapable of understanding in 1980 that their federal government had been struggling since 1968 for constitutional reform that was very different from that advocated by the separatist party is to do them an injustice.

And Mr. Morin is guilty of committing precisely that injustice. Wanting to impute my motives, Mr. Morin reveals to us his own thinking when he states that "Mr. Lévesque and other political 'initiates' knew how to 'decode'" Trudeau's hidden objectives. Then postulating that the "'uneducated' . . . had over a long period of time been unable to understand (me)," he concludes that I wanted to trick these "'uneducated' . . . (who) comprised a bigger and more influencable part of the electorate than the 'initiates.'"

(Mr. Adam makes the same distinction between the "initiates in constitutional matters" who would have understood me, and "the majority of Quebecers (who) pay scant attention to constitutional debate.")

There, in brief, is the entire argument of those who lost the 1980 referendum. The "uneducated" (the expression occurs three times in Mr. Morin's article) were not clever enough to understand that the constitutional reform that had been endlessly advocated since 1968 by our government would be the very reform we'd be introducing if we won the referendum.

Consequently, in voting "no," the people of Quebec made a mistake — or, more precisely, these poor "uneducated" were deceived, the victims of "fraud" and of a "power play." All of which means that your daughter's a dummy and the separatists didn't really lose the referendum. And as the next consequence, the Meech Lake Accord is nothing more than a kind of reparation due to Quebecers — these good people who, in the eyes of the nationalists, are so vulnerable that they have to be granted special status in order to survive.

Such contempt for the people of Quebec!

And such contempt, too, for the elected representatives of Quebec, since they, too, would not have understood what Mr. Morin calls "the perverse results of the post-referendum constitutional arrangements."

Let's remember that the Members of Parliament from Quebec had voted in favour of the 1982 Constitution by 73 to 2 (vote of December 2, 1981). And the members of the legislative assembly from Quebec had voted 70 to 38 that they could not "accept the plan for repatriating the Constitution" (vote of December 1, 1981). If I am not mistaken, this makes a total of 72 delegates who did not accept the 1982 Constitution and a total of 111 who did accept it. What an amazing power play that was: one that was accepted by 60 per cent of Quebec's elected representatives!

So much for Mr. Morin. As for Mr. Adam, in his article of March 11, he does state that he is "imputing motives . . . and (he knows) that's rather despicable." Not that it prevents him from doing that very thing in his article of March 14, when he espouses Mr. Mulroney's view:

> Do you suppose for a moment that Mr. Trudeau and his colleagues would have proceeded to repatriate the Constitution in 1981-82 without the consent of Queen's Park (Ontario)?

Frankly, I don't know — and neither do Messrs. Mulroney and Adam. But I do know that it's despicable to condemn me by inventing historical might-have-beens. At least, if history is going to be written hypothetically, let the hypotheses be honest.

If the Ontario provincial government had obstructed all attempts since 1927 to repatriate the Constitution, if that government in 1964 and 1971 had withdrawn its support for a repatriation formula that it had itself proposed or accepted, if it had been told by the Supreme Court that it had no constitutional veto, if that government was the one that wanted Canada broken apart and had just lost a referendum on this issue, if more than 95 per cent of Ontario's Members of Parliament had supported a constitutional reform that Quebec and the eight other provinces wanted, why, yes! I believe we would have proceeded without the approval of Queen's Park.

But clearly, as the Viennese say, if my grandmother had wheels, she'd be a bloody bus! As you well know, Sir, that's no way to write history . . .

Let's Try to Have Done with May 1980

Claude Morin in La Presse, *Montreal, Tuesday, March 28, 1989:*

You'll allow me a few comments on Mr. Trudeau's reply in *La Presse* on March 22, following my article of the 14th.

According to him, I abbreviated his referendum promises of May 1980 by omitting the part that referred to the other provinces. Now, I was dealing with his commitments to Quebecers and I made that clear.

Since we're referring to the other provinces, let's talk about them. How could Mr. Trudeau imagine being able to impose his own plans on them after a referendum held in Quebec which, among other things, had to do with sovereignty-association but not with his version of federalism? By using one of his typical shortcuts, the former prime minister seemed to conclude that a "no" automatically meant Quebecers held with his personal concept of Canada. Even within this bizarre hypothesis, why would such a vote have made the other provinces submit to this?

Had this same "no" vote perhaps upset the normal workings of federalism and entitled Mr. Trudeau to alarm everyone? A "yes" would, however, have given the Quebec government only the mandate to negotiate sovereignty-association; it would not necessarily have made the other provinces give in to Quebec's demands. Those were the rules, as everyone knew (Mr. Trudeau best of all, as we were told repeatedly!). So why would a "no" have magically conferred on him the right to have his own way and obliged the other provinces to accept this? How could he derive the notion of unilateral action from the "no" but not from a "yes"?

Did the referendum result bring us support from the other provinces? Surely not, by virtue of Mr. Trudeau's words — as prime minister, he could not make commitments on their behalf — or, moreover, by virtue of their premiers' promises. Although they came to Quebec to affirm that a "no" vote would mean reforms to federalism that were more favourable to the Quebec entity, subsequent events revealed that they did not keep their promises — and that Mr. Trudeau surpassed them: he deduced from the referendum political trends that were not there.

The former prime minister, furthermore, has gone on to confuse *genres*. He says that in our administration, the Quebec entity expresses itself politically by way of both the Quebec government and the central government. Correct, save for one important nuance: each of these governments has its own powers. Neither may direct the other in its operation; neither may reduce the powers of the other without its consent. Quebec's federal ministers and delegates deal with federal matters and their provincial colleagues with Quebec's concerns. Ottawa may not speak, make commitments, or act on behalf of the provinces. To change this would mean altering the Constitution.

This is why I am not impressed by his argument that Quebec's federal delegates, in any case bound by party discipline, mainly favoured his constitutional approach of 1980-81. On the other hand, I'm intrigued that his own party, the federal Liberal party, along with the provincial Liberal party, now both favour the Meech Lake Accord. When were these two parties being forthright? In 1980-81, when they urged the Quebec government to ratify a reform made without its assent, in spite of (federal) commitments, or today when, in retrospect, they find that reform so unacceptable that they want to see it tidied up?

That said, if Mr. Trudeau's referendum commitments had meant, as he now claims, to reform the Constitution "in the way that (he) had literally been preaching since 1968," why did he express himself in a way that most people misunderstood — perhaps even taking it for a welcome political turnaround on his part? Why did the "no" side subsequently use his commitments to make people believe that a "no" would lead to a satisfactory resolution of Quebec's traditional demands on constitutional matters? And why, given this "misinterpretation," didn't Mr. Trudeau hasten to clarify matters by making another major statement?

Clearly, a lot more could be said, but let's look at something more useful to the dispute than a series of articles in *La Presse*. On the subject of the post-referendum events alone, I was compelled to write a book that is 395 pages long: *Lendemains piégés*, which contains a detailed exposition of facts that can be verified, along with (reproductions of) many relevant documents.

Rumour has it that Mr. Trudeau is now preparing his memoirs, or something of the sort. So much the better! I very much hope this is true. Let him present us with his own documented account of the facts. And let him explain to us by what apparent aberration, on the heels of what unaccountable train of events, an astonishing political heresy suddenly arose in 1987, in loyal quarters as federalist as his own party (oh, yes), and including provincial Liberals, Conservatives, the federal NDP, and the premiers of seven English-speaking provinces. For all of them supported a constitutional accord, that of Meech Lake, which may be deficient and even deceptive in many respects, but which squarely contradicts the Canadian federalist view extolled by Mr. Trudeau and his 1980-81 Acts.

I, for one, am anxious to learn how he alone can be right while all these other people still fail to understand that they are wrong.

A Last Word from Pierre Elliot Trudeau

Pierre Elliot Trudeau:

Claude Morin's article in *La Presse* of March 29, 1989 was not brought to my attention until mid-April — a little late for me to follow up with a reply, even if I had been tempted to do so.

But when Don Johnston told me that he planned to include that article in the Appendix of the present book, I thought I might allow myself to add the following reflections:

Mr. Morin affirms that my appeal to the other provinces in my last pre-referendum speech did not justify my making them "accept (my) version" of constitutional reform.

What a hollow argument that is! My appeal to the other provinces was certainly not to obtain a mandate that would permit me to impose my concepts for the Constitution on anybody, but rather to let all sides know up front that a "no" victory would be taken as a mandate to bring to a conclusion the constitutional negotiations begun in 1927, that several provincial premiers were still saying in 1979 there was no hurry to complete.

Secondly, Mr. Morin attacks my evidence that there was

"a total of 72 delegates (from Quebec) who did not accept the 1982 Constitution (versus) a total of 111 who did": he boldly asserts that this evidence does not justify "Ottawa (to) behave as if it could speak, make commitments, or act on behalf of the provinces."

Still another hollow argument! The evidence in question has no other purpose than to show that the 1982 Constitution was not perceived as a "power play" by 60 per cent of Quebec's elected delegates.

If our federal government had simply wanted to force the provinces to submit to its wishes, if it had claimed the right to "speak, make commitments, or act" on their behalf, would it have undertaken, from 1968 to 1982, 14 long years of negotiations? Would it, in November 1981 — after 18 months of uninterrupted negotiations — have made the concessions to the provinces that were needed to obtain the consensus as defined by the Supreme Court, by accepting the "notwithstanding" clause and a hybrid formula for constitutional amendment?

Throughout his *Lendemains piégés*, Mr. Morin has described for us the essence of the matter. Chief negotiator for the P.Q. government and hence, privileged witness to that government's attitude during the post-referendum negotiations, he writes:

How to lead people to believe that they (i.e. the P.Q. negotiators) really sought to improve federalism when the party in power (the Parti Québécois) had always asserted that the (federal) administration could not be transformed but would have to be replaced? (p. 17)

What was most important . . . (was) to prove once more that it is futile to hope for anything from those who have no wish to offer anything. And if the impossible happened, and the federalists did have something worthwhile to propose, why not just go along with it and consider it as an instalment toward sovereignty? (p. 19)

The accord of April 16 (1981 — among the eight provinces opposed to repatriation and to the Charter) . . . in itself represented the maximum of any concessions Quebec could make. Its only goal in joining this opposition was to block a federal plan . . . (p. 282)

Aren't these admissions of bad faith in negotiations, and wouldn't it have been more forthright for the Quebec government to have declared from the start — at the first meeting in June 1980 — that it had no intention of accepting any federal reform that would not fit in with sovereignty-association?

Yet even today, these are the nationalists who act like violated virgins and claim that the federal government did the deed. Now, even a Mr. Pierre Fournier, professor of political science, is getting involved. In *La Presse* of March 17, 1989, he wrote that "the polls were categorical" in that they showed "the people" were opposed to repatriation; in support of his argument, he cites a poll of March 1981 (eight months before the accord in repatriation!) and another of March 1982.

I realize that I am no expert on polls and I know nothing of the background of the polls to which Mr. Fournier refers. But before talking about "categorical" results, I think the professor might have done some more thorough research. In the *Globe and Mail* of May 5, 1982 the results of a Sorecom poll were reported, affirming that at the end of January 1982: "most Quebecers believe that Premier René Lévesque should have signed (the November accord) once it had been modified"; the same poll showed that "almost three quarters of Quebecers believe that it is important for the province to be part of Canada."

In *La Presse* of June 19, 1982 a Gallup poll revealed that at the beginning of May, 49 per cent of Quebecers believed the Constitution of 17 April 1982 was a good thing for Canada, compared with 16 per cent who believed the opposite. Finally, on December 15, 1982, *La Presse* published the results of another Gallup poll, which showed that at the beginning of November 1982, 58 per cent of Quebecers believed that "Confederation would not break down," compared with 23 per cent who believed the opposite.

None of which would prevent the separatists and those of their henchmen who sit in the Senate and the Commons from claiming some years later that Quebecers had been thoroughly humiliated by the 1982 repatriation and that Meech Lake was essential as a kind of reparation to them.

In games of love and of luck, the rules are relentless; but their results are seldom known in advance, precisely because of the luck factor. The players are simply honour-bound not to cheat and to accept graciously their victory or their defeat.

In politics, the same applies. It means putting all your cards on the table and competing, so to speak, with your visor up. And trusting in chance as much as in skill. Now, during the long contest for repatriation of the Constitution that began in 1927 and was concluded in 1982, the stake was always power: that of the governments, that of the people. No one player could make a safe bet on the outcome, affected as it would be by the flux of election results; the consistency of alliances and interests; by the fluctuations in public opinion; or, above all, by the decisions of the courts.

Everyone was playing to win — but they all knew they might lose. And if they were unable to accept defeat, honour demanded that they should not be at the table.

It is said that René Lévesque was passionate about the gambling. I don't know how he played the game, but I wouldn't do him the injustice of imagining that he played with the attitude that loser takes all.

So! He played the referendum game and lost. He played the alliances game and lost. He played at negotiating and lost. He played the game of appealing to the courts and lost. He played the game of counting the votes of the

Quebec delegates (provincial and federal) and he lost.

Which did not prevent him, at the end of his career, from stating that federalism was a risk worth taking. In that, he showed himself to have more class than those who today call themselves victims of a constitutional power play.

As for me, I have no doubt whatsoever that if the "yes" side had won the 1980 referendum, I would have lost the confidence of Quebecers, and I would have had to resign. Moreover, I said so: if the sovereignty option prevailed, I must not be counted on to negotiate with Quebec; such a result would have meant the need for a new (federal) government with a new mandate.

I don't like (Quebec) nationalists because they are bad losers. The late president Harry Truman had some advice for such people: "If you can't stand the heat, get (sic) out of the kitchen." It is my impression that Quebec will never attain real stature so long as her political class is saddled with nationalists who are cry-babies and blackmailers.

Appendix A

Quebec 'a Major Winner'?

Following are translations of speeches by Premier Robert Bourassa in the Quebec National Assembly on June 18, 1987, and June 23, 1987.

. . . Mr. Speaker, there can be no doubt that Quebec has come out of the 1987 constitutional negotiations a major winner. The gains are substantial. For the first time in 120 years, the Constitution will recognize Quebec as a distinct society. It will at long last include Quebec in a place of honour: section 2 of the *Constitution Act* (1867).

The Constitution will give Quebec the means to preserve and promote our distinct identity and it will provide a constitutional foundation for the French fact in Quebec. The Constitution will guarantee Quebec the security it needs to develop within the federation. These are the powers we have obtained:

• increased powers over immigration;
• a voice in the appointment of judges to the Supreme Court of Canada;
• increased influence in the reform of federative institutions;
• two guarantees of a right to opt out, one with respect to the amending formula; the second with respect to the spending power.

If we look into this in greater detail, we see first of all that with the recognition of our distinct identity we have achieved a major gain, and one that is not merely symbolic, because the Constitution of our country must now be interpreted in accordance with this recognition.

The French language is a fundamental characteristic of our uniqueness, but there are other aspects, such as our culture and our institutions, whether political, economic or judicial. As we have so often said, we did not want a laboriously spelled-out definition, for the simple reason that it would confine and hamper the National Assembly in promoting this uniqueness. It must be noted that Quebec's distinct identity will be protected and promoted by the National Assembly and government, and its duality preserved by our legislators.

It cannot be stressed too strongly that the entire Constitution, including the Charter, will be interpreted and applied in the light of the section proclaiming our distinctness as a society. As a result, in the exercise of our legislative jurisdictions we will be able to consolidate what has already been achieved, and gain new ground.

With section 2 we have obtained sure and lasting constitutional means of consolidating our powers in the area of language. Thanks to the drafting of this section, and in particular its safeguard clause, the powers of the National Assembly are maintained and protected. There will be no further erosion of our jurisdiction over language. No regression will be possible. The protection is absolute, as I have so often told the Assembly. Our only path now is that of strengthening and consolidating the position of the French language.

The only limitations on our jurisdiction can be found in section 23 of the Charter and section 133 of the *Constitution Act* (1867). The right of recourse when necessary to section 33 of the Charter is integrally upheld. In short, and this is of the utmost importance, we have for the first time in

120 years of federalism managed to provide constitutional underpinnings for the preservation and promotion of the French character of Quebec.

With respect to immigration, which is obviously an area of jurisdiction of increasing importance to Quebec given the trends in our demography, we must preserve a delicate demographic balance. First, Quebec's desire to control its own immigration is recognized. Within Quebec, we want to preserve our demographic balance and our French-speaking identity. Outside Quebec, we want to see our proportion of the Canadian population maintained — this is crucial to our clout as a member of the Canadian federation. Quebec society, a minority in both Canada and North America, is different from the society that surrounds it, and we must have our hands on the levers that control immigration.

The growing number of new arrivals in Quebec must reinforce, not warp, our numerical importance.

The powers in this sector are decisive. Quebec has obtained a guarantee that it may if it wishes choose to receive the number of immigrants, out of the Canadian total, that corresponds to its proportion of the Canadian population plus 5%.

Quebec has also obtained the right to select the immigrants who want to come here, subject, naturally, to the general rules governing admission to Canada and Canadian policy on family reunification. Quebec will be solely responsible for the adaptation and integration of its immigrants.

With respect to the Supreme Court, Quebec as a distinct society wishes to ensure that it is adequately represented on the Court, which is the ultimate constitutional arbiter. The Court's constitutional status has been placed above and beyond the reach of a single level of government. Moreover, because of Canada's systems of law, Quebec sought appropriate representation on the Court, through a guarantee of three judges from this province and a voice in the selection and appointment of judges.

In the agreement of June 3, we obtained that guarantee of three judges, and a commitment from Ottawa that it would from now on choose them from a list of candidates submitted by the Quebec government.

With respect to the federal spending power, we have obtained the best possible framework for its exercise through a guarantee of flexibility and respect for provincial areas of jurisdiction. The exercise of the federal spending power has for the past 30 years been a zone of constant friction between the federal government and the provinces. Quebec has always vigorously denounced the unilateral exercise of this spending power, which has been the equivalent of actual constitutional amendments made *de facto* to the division of areas of legislative jurisdiction.

The June 3 Constitutional Accord represents a very significant step in the evolution of relations between Ottawa and the provincial governments because it profoundly alters the dynamic we have lived with up to the present. The introduction of the guaranteed right of a province preferring not to participate in a new shared-cost program, to opt out and receive fair financial compensation, is a major step forward. The right to opt out does not mean the end of national programs. It will mean that these programs will be designed with greater respect for the provinces, and that Quebec will have the flexibility it needs to implement measures and programs that, while compatible with national objectives, will more accurately reflect its own needs.

The definition of national objectives will, of course, have to be done in cooperation with the provinces, and we are assured that they will be defined within the normal framework of intergovernmental relations in Canada, that is, in the framework of the usual political negotiations.

We have taken special precautions to ensure that recognition of Quebec's right to opt out will not mean legal recognition of a federal right to set up programs in provincial areas of jurisdiction. The new section 106(a) is drafted so that it speaks solely of the right to opt out, without either recognizing or defining the federal spending power. To be doubly sure, we insisted on having a reserve or safeguard clause added, specifying that the legislative powers of the federal Parliament were not being extended. So Quebec keeps the right to contest before the courts any unconstitutional use of the spending power.

Lastly, we have gained recognition of our right of veto, our right to say No to any amendment that goes against the interests of Quebec. Constitutional gains would ring very hollow if the Constitution could once again be amended without Quebec's consent. We have covered all the angles, if I may put it like that. Quebec will be entitled to reasonable compensation whenever an amendment is made transferring powers from provincial legislatures to Parliament.

Quebec has a full veto over any change in the following areas: provincial representation in the House of Commons, Senate reform, certain aspects of the Supreme Court, extension of existing provinces into new territory and the creation of new provinces.

These in a nutshell are the benefits we have obtained. A committee of this House looked into Quebec's right to self-determination, and questions were raised about what would become of that right. Before the committee I told the leader of the Opposition that the Liberal Party of Quebec had recognized and still does recognize that right. By freely and voluntarily deciding to adhere to the *Constitution Act of 1982*, Quebec is expressing the right of its people to control their own destiny, as we did more explicitly in 1980, by choosing the Canadian option. In that respect, as in all other aspects of the Meech Lake Accord, there is thus no regression for Quebec, no renunciation, no decrease in our rights and prerogatives.

I would like to quote a resolution adopted by the Quebec Liberal Party. It is still in effect — it is part of our constitutional platform. It was adopted at the orientation conference in Montreal, held on February 29 and March 1 and 2, 1980, and at the general meeting at Saint-Hyacinthe on July 5 and 6, 1980, when the Minister of Education was leader of this

Party. The resolution states that the Liberal Party of Quebec recognizes Quebec's right to determine its internal constitution and to express freely its desire to maintain or to terminate the Canadian federal union. In short, it recognizes the right of the people of Quebec to determine freely their own future. This resolution was adopted in 1980 and has never been changed in the slightest. It is still part of our platform, and the adoption of the Meech Lake Accord makes no difference to it at all.

I have tried to give you an idea of the stride forward that adopting this resolution will accomplish. For 200 years, since the beginning of its history, Quebec has had to struggle. Our society, our people, have made considerable progress, especially since the start of the Quiet Revolution, and above all, over the past few decades, in the economic sector. With the adoption of this resolution we will have greater political stability. True patriotism is the patriotism that expresses itself in the desire to struggle and progress both individually and collectively.

The Meech Lake Accord is, in our opinion, one of the most splendid and powerful demonstrations of enlightened patriotism we have seen in this House since its history began. I am proud, and I feel sure my pride is shared by a very great majority of our fellow citizens.

From Canadian Parliamentary Review, Autumn 1987.

* * *

One should note that the conditions demanded by Quebec to adhere to the Canadian Constitution are clearly more important than the conditions laid down by the previous government (Parti Quebecois). Obviously we are very satisfied with the results. Quebec has been recognized for what it is, which has never happened before. Canada has understood and accepted that we must be recognized for what are, namely our distinct identity. There are three means necessary to remain what we are: control of our population through demographics, immigration and language; real control over funding in our areas of jurisdiction when the federal spending power comes into play; and a constitutional guarantee with respect to the interpretation of the Constitution which is now available, with gains achieved at the level of the Supreme Court. Finally, we have obtained an amending formula which will serve as an insurance policy with which to preserve our future . . .

We have obtained linguistic security. Language laws were adopted in 1974 and in 1977 and now with this safeguard provision (Section 2(4)), we are guaranteed that existing powers of Quebec cannot be affected (by the constitutional amendment). As well, there is the potential to obtain new powers as Quebec evolves in areas which will promote our culture, whether it be immigration, communication or other areas . . . Quebec has realized one of the most important political victories of its history, a victory recognized by most objective observers as one of its greatest in two hundred years.

For the first time we are the winners in a constitutional debate. All the provinces accepted all of our conditions. Who can claim a greater achievement in the constitutional history of Quebec?

I am convinced that it is a forward step to the advantage of Quebecers and of Canada. In his comments the leader of the [provincial] Opposition (Pierre-Marc Johnson) constantly referred to constitutional matters which have not yet been completely settled. Is he not forgetting that there will be a second round?. . . I cite his predecessor Monsieur René Lévesque who said . . . that there was one non-negotiable precondition, namely the recognition of the distinct people of Quebec. When the leader of the Opposition says that his government had never demanded so little, I would draw his attention to this declaration (of Lévesque) . . . We demanded

five times more than his government because we had five conditions, not only one.

But I say to the leader of the Opposition when he begins
to cite a number of areas not yet settled, there will be another
round of negotiations.

Unofficial translation by Editor. Words in parentheses added by Editor.

Appendix B

Meeting of First Ministers on the Constitution

1987 Constitutional Accord

June 3, 1987

WHEREAS first ministers, assembled in Ottawa, have arrived at a unanimous accord on constitutional amendments that would bring about the full and active participation of Quebec in Canada's constitutional evolution, would recognize the principle of equality of all the provinces, would provide new arrangements to foster greater harmony and cooperation between the Government of Canada and the governments of the provinces and would require that annual first ministers' conferences on the state of the Canadian economy and such other matters as may be appropriate be convened and that annual constitutional conferences composed of first ministers be convened commencing not later than December 31, 1988;

AND WHEREAS first ministers have also reached unanimous agreement on certain additional commitments in relation to some of those amendments;

NOW THEREFORE the Prime Minister of Canada and the first ministers of the provinces commit themselves and the governments they represent to the following:

1. The Prime Minister of Canada will lay or cause to be laid before the Senate and House of Commons, and the first ministers of the provinces will lay or cause to be laid before their legislative assemblies, as soon as possible, a resolution, in the form appended hereto, to authorize a proclamation to be issued by the Governor General under the Great Seal of Canada to amend the Constitution of Canada.

2. The Government of Canada will, as soon as possible, conclude an agreement with the Government of Quebec that would

(a) incorporate the principles of the Cullen-Couture agreement on the selection abroad and in Canada of independent immigrants, visitors for medical treatment, students and temporary workers, and on the selection of refugees abroad and economic criteria for family reunification and assisted relatives,

(b) guarantee that Quebec will receive a number of immigrants, including refugees, within the annual total established by the federal government for all of Canada proportionate to its share of the population of Canada, with the right to exceed that figure by five per cent for demographic reasons, and

(c) provide an undertaking by Canada to withdraw services (except citizenship services) for the reception and integration (including linguistic and cultural) of all foreign nationals wishing to settle in Quebec where services are to be provided by Quebec, with such withdrawal to be accompanied by reasonable compensation, and the Government of Canada and the Government of Quebec will take the necessary steps to give the agreement the force of law under the proposed amendment relating to such agreements.

3. Nothing in this Accord should be construed as preventing the negotiation of similar agreements with other provinces relating to immigration and the temporary admission of aliens.

4. Until the proposed amendment relating to appointments to the Senate comes into force, any person summoned to fill a vacancy in the Senate shall be chosen from among persons whose names have been submitted by the government of the province to which the vacancy relates and must be acceptable to the Queen's Privy Council for Canada.

Motion for a Resolution to authorize an amendment to the Constitution of Canada

WHEREAS the *Constitution Act, 1982* came into force on April 17, 1982, following an agreement between Canada and all the provinces except Quebec;

AND WHEREAS the Government of Quebec has established a set of five proposals for constitutional change and has stated that amendments to give effect to those proposals would enable Quebec to resume a full role in the constitutional councils of Canada;

AND WHEREAS the amendment proposed in the schedule hereto sets out the basis on which Quebec's five constitutional proposals may be met;

AND WHEREAS the amendment proposed in the schedule hereto also recognizes the principle of the equality of all the provinces, provides new arrangements to foster greater harmony and cooperation between the Government of Canada and the governments of the provinces and requires that conferences be convened to consider important constitutional, economic and other issues;

AND WHEREAS certain portions of the amendment proposed in the schedule hereto relate to matters referred to in section 41 of the *Constitution Act, 1982*;

AND WHEREAS section 41 of the *Constitution Act, 1982* provides that an amendment to the Constitution of Canada may be made by proclamation issued by the Governor General under the Great Seal of Canada where so authorized by resolutions of the Senate and the House of Commons and of the legislative assembly of each province;

NOW THEREFORE the (Senate) (House of Commons) (legislative assembly) resolves that an amendment to the Constitution of Canada be authorized to be made by proclamation issued by Her Excellency the Governor General under the Great Seal of Canada in accordance with the schedule hereto.

SCHEDULE

CONSTITUTION AMENDMENT, 1987

Constitution Act, 1867

1. The *Constitution Act, 1867* is amended by adding thereto, immediately after section 1 thereof, the following section:

Interpretation

''2.(1) The Constitution of Canada shall be interpreted in a manner consistent with

(a) the recognition that the existence of French-speaking Canadians, centred in Quebec but also present elsewhere in Canada, and English-speaking Canadians, concentrated outside Quebec but also present in Quebec, constitutes a fundamental characteristic of Canada; and

(b) the recognition that Quebec constitutes within Canada a distinct society.

Role of Parliament and legislature

(2) The role of the Parliament of Canada and the provincial legislatures to preserve the fundamental characteristic of Canada referred to in paragraph (1)(a) is affirmed.

Role of legislature and Government of Quebec

(3) The role of the legislature and Government of Quebec to preserve and promote the distinct identity of Quebec referred to in paragraph (1)(b) is affirmed.

Rights of legislatures and governments preserved

(4) Nothing in this section derogates from the powers, rights or privileges of Parliament or the Government of Canada, or of the legislatures or governments of the provinces, including any powers, rights or privileges relating to language.''

2. The said Act is further amended by adding thereto, immediately after section 24 thereof, the following section:

Names to be submitted

''25.(1) Where a vacancy occurs in the Senate, the government of the province to which the vacancy relates may, in relation to that vacancy, submit to the Queen's Privy Council for Canada the names of persons who may be summoned to the Senate.

Choice of Senators from names submitted

(2) Until an amendment to the Constitution of Canada is made in relation to the Senate pursuant to section 41 of the *Constitution Act*, *1982*, the person summoned to fill a vacancy in the Senate shall

be chosen from among persons whose names have been submitted under subsection (1) by the government of the province to which the vacancy relates and must be acceptable to the Queen's Privy Council for Canada.''

3. The said Act is further amended by adding thereto, immediately after section 95 thereof, the following heading and sections:

"Agreements on Immigration and Aliens

Commitment to negotiate	95A. The Government of Canada shall, at the request of the government of any province, negotiate with the government of that province for the purpose of concluding an agreement relating to immigration or the temporary admission of aliens into that province that is appropriate to the needs and circumstances of that province.
Agreements	95B.(1) Any agreement concluded between Canada and a province in relation to immigration or the temporary admission of aliens into that province has the force of law from the time it is declared to do so in accordance with subsection 95C (1) and shall from that time have effect notwithstanding class 25 of section 91 or section 95.
Limitation	(2) An agreement that has the force of law under subsection (1) shall have effect only so long and so far as it is not repugnant to any provision of an Act of the Parliament of Canada that sets national standards and objectives relating to immigration or aliens, including any provision that establishes general classes of immigrants or relates

to levels of immigration for Canada or that prescribes classes of individuals who are inadmissible into Canada.

Application of Charter

(3) The *Canadian Charter of Rights and Freedoms* applies in respect of any agreement that has the force of law under subsection (1) and in respect of anything done by the Parliament or Government of Canada, or the legislature or government of a province, pursuant to any such agreement.

Proclamation relating to agreements

95C.(1) A declaration that an agreement referred to in subsection 95B (1) has the force of law may be made by proclamation issued by the Governor General under the Great Seal of Canada only where so authorized by resolutions of the Senate and House of Commons and of the legislative assembly of the province that is a party to the agreement.

Amendment of agreements

(2) An amendment to an agreement referred to in subsection 95B (1) may be made by proclamation issued by the Governor General under the Great Seal of Canada only where so authorized

(a) by resolutions of the Senate and House of Commons and of the legislative assembly of the province that is a party to the agreement; or

(b) in such other manner as is set out in the agreement.

Application of sections 46 to 48 of

95D. Sections 46 to 48 of the *Constitution Act, 1982* apply, with such modifications as the circumstances require, in respect of any declaration made pursuant to subsection 95C (1), any amendment to an agreement made pursuant to subsection 95C (2) or any amendment made pursuant to section 95E.

95E. An amendment to sections 95A to 95D or this section may be made in accordance with the procedure set out in subsection 38(1) of the *Constitution Act, 1982*, but only if the amendment is authorized by resolutions of the legislative assemblies of all the provinces that are, at the time of the amendment, parties to an agreement that has the force of law under subsection 95B (1).''

4. The said Act is further amended by adding thereto, immediately preceding section 96 thereof, the following heading:

''General''

5. The said Act is further amended by adding thereto, immediately preceding section 101 thereof, the following heading:

''Courts Established by the Parliament of Canada''

6. The said Act is further amended by adding thereto, immediately after section 101 thereof, the following heading and sections:

''Supreme Court of Canada

101A.(1) The court existing under the name of the Supreme Court of Canada is hereby continued as the general court of appeal for Canada, and as an additional court for the better administration of the laws of Canada, and shall continue to be a superior court of record.

Constitution of court

(2) The Supreme Court of Canada shall consist of a chief justice to be called the Chief Justice of Canada and eight other judges, who shall be appointed by the Governor General in Council by letters patent under the Great Seal.

Who may be appointed judges

101B.(1) Any person may be appointed a judge of the Supreme Court of Canada who, after having been admitted to the bar of any province or territory, has, for a total of at least ten years, been a judge of any court in Canada or a member of the bar of any province or territory.

Three judges from Quebec

(2) At least three judges of the Supreme Court of Canada shall be appointed from among persons who, after having been admitted to the bar of Quebec, have, for a total of at least ten years, been judges of any court of Quebec or of any court established by the Parliament of Canada, or members of the bar of Quebec.

Names may be submitted

101C.(1) Where a vacancy occurs in the Supreme Court of Canada, the government of each province may, in relation to that vacancy, submit to the Minister of Justice of Canada the names of any of the persons who have been admitted to the bar of that province and are qualified under section 101B for appointment to that court.

Appointment from names submitted	(2) Where an appointment is made to the Supreme Court of Canada, the Governor General in Council shall, except where the Chief Justice is appointed from among members of the Court, appoint a person whose name has been submitted under subsection (1) and who is acceptable to the Queen's Privy Council for Canada.
Appointment from Quebec	(3) Where an appointment is made in accordance with subsection (2) of any of the three judges necessary to meet the requirement set out in subsection 101B (2), the Governor General in Council shall appoint a person whose name has been submitted by the Government of Quebec.
Appointment from other provinces	(4) Where an appointment is made in accordance with subsection (2) otherwise than as required under subsection (3), the Governor General in Council shall appoint a person whose name has been submitted by the government of a province other than Quebec.
Tenure, salaries, etc. of judges	101D. Sections 99 and 100 apply in respect of the judges of the Supreme Court of Canada.
Relationship to section 101	101E.(1) Sections 101A to 101D shall not be construed as abrogating or derogating from the powers of the Parliament of Canada to make laws under section 101 except to the extent that such laws are inconsistent with those sections.

References
to the
Supreme Court
of Canada

(2) For greater certainty, section 101A shall not be construed as abrogating or derogating from the powers of the Parliament of Canada to make laws relating to the reference of questions of law or fact, or any other matters, to the Supreme Court of Canada.''

7. The said Act is further amended by adding thereto, immediately after section 106 thereof, the following section:

Shared-cost
program

''106A.(1) The Government of Canada shall provide reasonable compensation to the government of a province that chooses not to participate in a national shared-cost program that is established by the Government of Canada after the coming into force of this section in an area of exclusive provincial jurisdiction, if the province carries on a program or initiative that is compatible with the national objectives.

Legislative
power not
extended

(2) Nothing in this section extends the legislative powers of the Parliament of Canada or of the legislatures of the provinces.''

8. The said Act is further amended by adding thereto the following heading and sections:

''XII — CONFERENCES ON THE ECONOMY AND OTHER MATTERS

Conferences
on the
economy and
other matters

148. A conference composed of the Prime Minister of Canada and the first ministers of the provinces shall be convened by the Prime Minister of Canada at least once each

year to discuss the state of the Canadian economy and such other matters as may be appropriate.

XIII — REFERENCES

Reference includes amendments

149. A reference to this Act shall be deemed to include a reference to any amendments thereto.''

Constitution Act, 1982

9. Sections 40 to 42 of the *Constitution Act, 1982* are repealed and the following substituted therefor:

Compensation

''40. Where an amendment is made under subsection 38(1) that transfers legislative powers from provincial legislatures to Parliament, Canada shall provide reasonable compensation to any province to which the amendment does not apply.

Amendment by unanimous consent

41. An amendment to the Constitution of Canada in relation to the following matters may be made by proclamation issued by the Governor General under the Great Seal of Canada only where authorized by resolutions of the Senate and House of Commons and of the legislative assembly of each province:

(a) the office of the Queen, the Governor General and the Lieutenant Governor of a province;
(b) the powers of the Senate and the method of selecting Senators;
(c) the number of members by which a province is entitled to be represented in

the Senate and the residence qualifications of Senators;

(*d*) the right of a province to a number of members in the House of Commons not less than the number of Senators by which the province was entitled to be represented on *April 17, 1982*;

(*e*) the principle of proportionate representation of the provinces in the House of Commons prescribed by the Constitution of Canada;

(*f*) subject to section 43, the use of the English or the French language;

(*g*) the Supreme Court of Canada;

(*h*) the extension of existing provinces into the territories;

(*i*) notwithstanding any other law or practice, the establishment of new provinces; and

(*j*) an amendment to this Part.''

10. Section 44 of the said Act is repealed and the following substituted therefor:

Amendments
by
Parliament

''44. Subject to section 41, Parliament may exclusively make laws amending the Constitution of Canada in relation to the executive government of Canada or the Senate and House of Commons.''

11. Subsection 46(1) of the said Act is repealed and the following substituted therefor:

Initiation
of amendment
procedures

''46.(1) The procedures for amendment under sections 38, 41 and 43 may be initiated either by the Senate or the House of Commons or by the legislative assembly of a province.''

12. Subsection 47(1) of the said Act is repealed and the following substituted therefor:

Amendments
without
Senate
resolution

"47.(1) An amendment to the Constitution of Canada made by proclamation under section 38, 41 or 43 may be made without a resolution of the Senate authorizing the issue of the proclamation if, within one hundred and eighty days after the adoption by the House of Commons of a resolution authorizing its issue, the Senate has not adopted such a resolution and if, at any time after the expiration of that period, the House of Commons again adopts the resolution."

13. Part VI of the said Act is repealed and the following substituted therefor:

"PART VI
CONSTITUTIONAL CONFERENCES

Constitutional
conference

50.(1) A constitutional conference composed of the Prime Minister of Canada and the first ministers of the provinces shall be convened by the Prime Minister of Canada at least once each year, commencing in 1988.

Agenda

(2) The conferences convened under subsection (1) shall have included on their agenda the following matters:

(a) Senate reform, including the role and functions of the Senate, its powers, the method of selecting Senators and representation in the Senate;

(b) roles and responsibilities in relation to fisheries; and

(c) such other matters as are agreed upon.''

14. Subsection 52(2) of the said Act is amended by striking out the word ''and'' at the end of paragraph (b) thereof, by adding the word ''and'' at the end of paragraph (c) thereof and by adding thereto the following paragraph:

''(d) any other amendment to the Constitution of Canada.''

15. Section 61 of the said Act is repealed and the following substituted therefor:

References

''61. *A reference to the Constitution Act 1982, or* a reference to the *Constitution Acts 1867 to 1982*, shall be deemed to include a reference to *any amendments thereto.*''

General

Multicultural heritage and aboriginal peoples

16. Nothing in section 2 of the *Constitution Act, 1867* affects section 25 or 27 of the *Canadian Charter of Rights and Freedoms*, section 35 of the *Constitution Act, 1982* or class 24 of section 91 of the *Constitution Act, 1867*.

CITATION

Citation

17. This amendment may be cited as the *Constitution Amendment, 1987*.

Signed at Ottawa,
June 3, 1987

Fait à Ottawa
le 3 juin 1987

Notes

[1] The final language in section 2 (1) (a) of the Constitutional Accord was changed to refer to "French-speaking *Canadians*" and "English-speaking *Canadians*" rather than French-speaking or English-speaking Canada as in the original Meech Lake agreement. As numerous experts have noted, however, the new wording will still lead to the eventual emergence of two territorially-based unilingual Canadas.

[2] See note 23 for an explanation of the notwithstanding clause. The origins of this clause lie in the pressure from the eight premiers who opposed the Charter of Rights and other aspects of the 1980 patriation proposal of the Federal government. The leaders of this so-called "gang of eight" were Sterling Lyon of Manitoba and Allan Blakeney of Saskatchewan. They opposed the Charter because they believed in the primacy of Parliament and the provincial legislatures as the sole defenders of individual rights. In their view, provincial legislative powers would be unacceptably undermined by giving the people of Canada the power to strike down legislation through the courts.

[3] See the Constitutional Accord, Appendix C. The provinces gain from the federal government the right to opt out of future national shared-cost programs with full compensation (section 106A), potential control over immigration into their respective provinces (section 95A-E), the power to nominate Supreme Court Justices (section 101) and Senators (section 25) and an extended veto power over future changes to the Constitution (section 41). In addition, the Charter is undermined by the Accord through the combined effect of section 2 and section 16 of the Constitution Amendment. Experts say this will allow the Quebec government to override the Charter and will create a hierarchy of rights among Canadians.

Finally, the Accord constitutionally entrenches First Ministers' Conferences (section 148) and specifies that the agenda of the annual constitutional conference must deal with provincial demands on Senate reform and the jurisdiction over Fisheries (section 50).

[4] The introduction of the Fulton-Favreau constitutional package into Quebec's National Assembly on October 30, 1964 led to heated constitutional debate. Premier Jean Lesage finally "put off indefinitely" the National Assembly's consideration of the motion. Not long after, in 1966, Lesage's government fell to the Union Nationale. (See note 30 for a summary description of the Fulton-Favreau formula.)

[5] Robert Bourassa submitted the Victoria Charter to his Cabinet on June 21, 1971. But in the face of mounting criticism, he abandoned his support on the grounds that the Victoria Charter could not meet the needs of the people of Quebec which required an even more decentralized federal system.

[6] See pages 54 to 62.

[7] The Supreme Court judgment handed down on September 28, 1981 found that although no provincial consent was required by law, "substantial" provincial consent was necessary by convention. The Court did not define "substantial" but it did state that two provinces were not enough.

[8] On December 6, 1982 the Supreme Court of Canada delivered a judgment which found that the convention had now been observed with nine provinces out of 10 supporting the patriation and that Quebec did not have a veto.

[9] Premier Bourassa answered the PQ's charge of "not enough" by saying that there would be a second round where

presumably he would continue to press for additional powers to Quebec. (See *Proceedings of the National Assembly*, p.9031, June 23, 1987.)

[10] See history of efforts by previous Prime Ministers, pages 41 to 46.

[11] Section 25, Appendix C.

[12] Ibid, section 101A-E.

[13] Ibid, sections 148 and 50.

[14] Interprovincial conferences are held each year under the chairmanship of a different premier. The first interprovincial conference was in 1887. The 1987 conference was held in St. John, New Brunswick from August 26 to 28 under the chairmanship of Richard Hatfield and the 1988 Conference was in Saskatoon, Saskatchewan on August 18 and 19 under the chairmanship of Grant Devine.

[15] See Section 95A-E, in Appendix C. This is a complex amendment which allows all the provinces to secure agreements with the federal government concerning provincial control over the admission and integration of immigrants into that province.

[16] Once an agreement has been entered into with a province, it cannot be terminated or changed without a resolution of the legislature of that province. Therefore the paramount role of the federal government in matters of immigration would be eliminated.

[17] See Section 106A, Appendix C. Under the present Constitution, the provinces enjoy exclusive jurisdiction in many matters that affect health, welfare, housing, education and

training. But the federal government has played an important role in these areas in trying to ensure minimum national standards of services to all Canadians regardless of provincial residence,through the use of the spending power. Medicare is an example with which most Canadians are familiar. Under the Canada Health Act of 1984, funds are transferred from the Federal Treasury to the provincial treasuries for the purposes of health insurance, one of the conditions being that extra billing by medical practitioners be curtailed. It would appear that under Meech Lake, the capacity of the federal government to stipulate such conditions would be eliminated and provinces would be free to take federal tax dollars and spend them on programs of their own design without adhering to national standards.

[18] See Section 41, Appendix C. In one way or another, the proposed amendment subjects all significant constitutional amendments in future to the unanimity rule. Alternatively, provision is made for the withdrawal of provinces from the application of amendments transferring legislative powers to Parliament, with compensation from the federal treasury. See Section 40, Appendix C.

[19] See Section 2, Appendix C.

[20] See The Report of the Special Joint Committee of the Senate and the House of Commons on the 1987 Constitutional Accord.

[21] Senator Lowell Murray, Minister of Federal-Provincial Relations.

[22] Section 40 of the Constitution Act of 1982 permitted a province to opt out of an amendment to the Constitution which transferred powers to the federal government. However, unless the transfer related to education or cultural matters

(to accommodate the province of Quebec), no compensation would be payable to a province taking advantage of the opting-out provision. Under the proposed Constitutional Accord of 1987, full compensation would be paid to any province opting out of any transfer of legislative power to Parliament (See section 40, Appendix C).

[23] Section 33 of the Constitution Act of 1982 provided that a province could suspend the application of Section 2 or Sections 7 through 15 of the Charter of Rights by a specific reference in a law adopted by a provincial legislative assembly. The suspension could have an effect for only five years, at which time it would have to be re-enacted to continue in force. This provision was demanded by most of the provinces in order to include their signatures on the November 5, 1981 agreement to patriate the Constitution.

[24] The Balfour Report was issued from a sub-committee of the Imperial Conference of 1926 which proposed the autonomy of the Commonwealth Dominions within the British Empire. The direct result of this was the passage of the Statute of Westminster in 1931 which gave complete legal autonomy to the countries of the Commonwealth. Unfortunately Canada could not claim its full autonomy because the original framers of the Constitution of 1867 had overlooked the need for a domestic amending formula and because the necessary consensus to formulate one was not achieved at the 1927 Dominion-Provincial Conference.

[25] Unemployment Insurance was introduced in 1940 after Britain sanctioned a constitutional amendment which allowed the federal government to establish a national insurance scheme.

[26] On December 16, 1949 the BNA Act was amended by the British Parliament at the request of the St. Laurent govern-

ment. The amendment to section 91 gave the federal Parliament the power to amend the Constitution in matters affecting federal power only.

27 Appeals to the Judicial Committee of the Privy Council in London were stopped in 1949 and the highest court of appeal in Canada became the Supreme Court.

28 The Canadian Bill of Rights was given Royal Assent on August 10, 1960. Prime Minister Diefenbaker would have preferred a constitutional amendment for the protection of individual rights, but it was felt at the time that the provincial unanimity needed for the constitutional entrenchment of the Bill would have been impossible. For this reason the Bill remained a federal statute and it applies only to federal laws.

29 The Royal Commission on Bilingualism and Biculturalism was commissioned on July 11, 1963 and the Report was submitted on October 8, 1967.

30 The Fulton-Favreau formula proposed that the federal government limit its power, acquired in 1949, to amend the Constitution to matters dealing with the Senate, the House of Commons and the Executive of the government. More general amendments concerning the status of the Queen in Canada, regional representation, and language use would be accomplished by an agreement of the federal government and two-thirds of the provinces representing 50 per cent of the population. However, any constitutional amendment to provincial jurisdiction would require unanimous consent of all the provinces. To counter this rigidity there was a reciprocal delegation provision which permitted the transfer of legislative powers between any four provinces and the federal government.

[31] Daniel Johnson was chosen leader of the Union Nationale Party in 1961 and became Premier of Quebec in 1966. His work *Egalité ou indépendance* is a clear statement of the "Two Nation" concept of Canada and guided the thinking of his government on constitutional reform.

[32] John Robarts was the Conservative Premier of Ontario from 1961 to 1967 and chaired the Confederation for Tomorrow Conference. After retiring, he continued his interest in constitutional matters and co-chaired the Task Force on Canadian Unity.

[33] The Confederation for Tomorrow Conference was convened by Ontario Premier John Robarts in November 1967.

[34] At the Victoria Conference of First Ministers in 1971 under the chairmanship of Prime Minister Trudeau, an agreement was reached on an amending formula. It stipulated that general constitutional amendments required the approval of Ontario, Quebec, two western provinces and two eastern provinces. This ensured a veto to Quebec. However, shortly after the termination of the conference, Premier Bourassa withdrew his consent. (See note 5.)

[35] The Alberta amending formula drew on the Fulton-Favreau formula: two-thirds of the provinces representing 50 per cent of the population for certain classes of amendments. Unanimity would prevail for any changes to provincial powers. This formula included an "opting-out" provision which allowed a province to opt out, with compensation, of any constitutional amendment which affected its jurisdiction. (See note 22).

[36] The "gang of eight" consisted of all provinces except Ontario and New Brunswick, these latter having agreed to proceed with the patriation as proposed.

[37] See note 7 regarding the judgment of the Supreme Court.

[38] Some changes in wording were hammered out between First Ministers.

[39] Quebec's five demands were first unveiled by Quebec Inter-governmental Affairs Minister Gil Rémillard at a Mont Gabriel Conference in May 1986. See Introduction, page 5.

[40] See note 8 concerning the Supreme Court decision of December 1982.

[41] See note 34 concerning the Victoria Charter.

[42] See note 22.

[43] Mr. Trudeau's offer to limit the federal spending power was made during a series of constitutional discussions that led to the Victoria Charter in 1971.

[44] Gilles Grégoire was a Quebec Social Credit MP in the 1960s.

[45] All three agreements were signed between the government of Quebec and the federal government. In May 1971, Immigration Minister Otto Lang signed an agreement with the province of Quebec that allowed Quebec immigration officials to have offices in certain federal immigration offices abroad. In October 1975, Immigration Minister Robert Andras signed an agreement with the province of Quebec that allowed for greater Quebec participation in the recruit-ment and selection of immigrants into Canada. In February 1978, Immigration Minister Bud Cullen signed an agreement with the province of Quebec that allowed the government of Quebec to jointly decide with the federal government those individuals who would immigrate to Quebec.

46 Until 1949 the Judicial Committee of Britain's Privy Council was the highest court of appeal for Canada. The Committee's perspective on Canadian federalism had a decidedly provincial bias, and the Committee's decisions significantly weakened federal powers and shifted the federal-provincial balance in favour of the provinces.

47 In the 1987 Annual Report, Canada's Commissioner of Official Languages, d'Iberville Fortier, had described Quebec's English-speaking minority as feeling "humiliated" because of Quebec's language policies. Subsequently, a unanimous resolution of the Quebec National Assembly condemned the commissioner and purported to tell English-speaking minorities how they should feel about Quebec's language laws.

48 See Appendix C.

49 Here Pierre Trudeau points out that the allocation of legislative powers not specifically dealt with in the Constitution, therefore left in the grey area between federal or provincial jurisdiction, depends on judicial interpretation. For example, aviation and broadcasting now fall under federal jurisdiction by virtue of judicial interpretation, not the formal language of the Constitution. Clearly the designation of Quebec as a "distinct society" with a special role to preserve and promote its "distinct identity" will significantly affect any future judicial interpretation of where to allocate legislative powers and of the relative scope of federal and provincial jurisdictions, such as in respect of communications.

50 See *Proceedings of The National Assembly*, Appendix B.

51 See Gil Rémillard's address to the National Assembly in the *Proceedings of the National Assembly*, June 19, 1987.

[52] *Winnipeg Free Press*, June 9, 1987.

[53] Yves Fortier, before the Joint Committee on the Constitutional Accord, August 25, 1987, page 81.

[54] Ibid.

[55] Pierre Marc Johnson, in the Quebec National Assembly, June 18, 1987.

[56] Jacques Parizeau, the successor to Johnson as leader of the Parti Québécois, March 18, 1988. Mr. Parizeau was Minister of Finance in the Lévesque government from 1976 to 1984.

[57] See 1987 Report of the Commissioner of Official Languages. According to the Report, outside Quebec, 224,120 students are enrolled in French immersion classes.